GETTING SCHOOLED ON RESISTANCE

An Exploration of Clashing Narratives in Urban School Reform

CYNTHIA D. URBANSKI, PhD

Synergy Publishing Group
Belmont, North Carolina

Published by Synergy Publishing Group, Belmont, NC

Cover by Arielle Torkelson
Interior Layout & Production by Melisa Graham

Second edition
Softcover, February 2024, ISBN 978-1-960892-12-6
E-book, February 2024, 978-1-960892-13-3

Library of Congress Control Number: 2024901618

First edition published in 2016 by Teacher's Press under the title *Untangling Urban Middle School Reform.*

To my children and resistant students and teachers everywhere.

ACKNOWLEDGEMENTS

I would like to acknowledge Dr. Lil Brannon for being always available to read drafts, think with me, and push me. I would also like to acknowledge Lacy Manship and my Writing Project site for working with me at Rosa Parks Middle School (an alias) and making my access to that school possible. Finally, I would like to acknowledge the administrators, teachers, and students at Rosa Parks Middle School for opening their classrooms and lives to me, and for telling me their stories.[1]

---

1 This work was based on the research from my dissertation, *Getting Schooled on Resistance: Dominant and Counter Narratives of Writing and the Circulation of Power in Urban School Reform.*

CONTENTS

FOREWORD 1

PREFACE 3

PART I: MAPPING CONFLICTING NARRATIVES

1: INTRODUCING THE POWER IN STORY AND THE STORY OF POWER 7

    Rosa Parks Middle School and the Writing Project 9

    Urban School Reform, Testing, and Accountability 12

    Reframing the Story and Framing the Book 14

2: ROSA PARKS MIDDLE SCHOOL 19

    Contrasting and Conflicting Stories 19

    Figuring the Story 20

    Rosa Parks Middle School from Our Outsider/Consultant Perspective 22

    Rosa Parks Middle School through the Administrators' Eyes 33

    Moving Toward Analysis 36

3: MAPPING SOCIAL REPRODUCTION 41

    Activity Theory and Figured Worlds: Tools for Analysis 43

    School Uniforms: Inscribing Narrative Theories-in-use on Students' Bodies 46

    Planning Meetings: Order and Control over Teachers 50

    Negotiating Narratives to "Be" Teacher or Student 55

PART II: HOW TO "BE" WRITING TEACHERS AND STUDENTS

4: NARROWING THE LENS 61

    A Word About Genre Theory: What We Were Attempting to Do 62

    Narratives of Convergence and Resistance 64

    Theories for Constructing Identities 65

    Competing Narratives of Writing 67

    Diary Writing: A Narrative of Convergence 69

    Daybook Writing: Narratives of Resistance and Compliance 72

    Negotiating Good Teacher Identities in a Complex World 75

5: REPRODUCING "GOOD STUDENT" WRITING 79
    Critical Discourse Analysis: A Micro Analysis of Language and Identity 81
    Leslie: Good Student Writers Repeat 82
    Erin: Good Students Try to Recreate Success 86
    Abigail: Good Students Test Well 93
    Reproducing Good "At-Risk" Student 97

6: BEING "BAD" 101
    Jada: Resisting through Innovation 102
    Trying On the American Dream 104
    Taking a Quiz 107
    Moments of Possibility 110

7: CONCLUSION 113
    Clashing Narratives and Power: a Recap 115
    Agency: Room for Change 116
    Steps Toward Change 118
    Images of Hope 119
    Getting Schooled on Resistance: Conclusions 120

ABOUT THE AUTHOR 122

APPENDIXES 123
    Appendix A: Gee's Critical Discourse Analysis 123
    Appendix B: Leslie's Interview in Stanzas 124
    Appendix C: Erin's Holocaust Diary Interview in Stanzas 124
    Appendix D: Erin's Second Interview in Stanzas 125
    Appendix E: Abigail's First Interview in Stanzas 125
    Appendix F: Abigail's Second Interview in Stanzas 126
    Appendix G: Jada's First Interview in Stanzas 126
    Appendix H: Jada's Second Interview in Stanzas 127
    Appendix I: Questions for Discussion Between Administrators,
        Teachers, and Consultants 128

REFERENCES 130

INDEX 133

FOREWORD

Progress moves at the speed of trust.
—Steven M. R. Covey (Covey & Merrill, 2008)

Life in schools is shaped as much by trust, or the lack of it, as anything else. After all, the variable of trust is central to the very enterprise of schooling, coloring the relationships that surround learning. Parents need to trust that schools have their children's best interests at heart if they are to commit to working in partnership. Teachers, administrators, and consultants need to trust one another if they are to pursue new visions of education that will better serve their students and communities. And above all, students need to trust that all these adults are really on their side as they navigate the increasingly complex pathway to adulthood. When trust is high, teachers and students alike risk pursuit of more ambitious learning, challenge their assumptions and work through disagreements, and hold themselves accountable to one another. When trust is low, these same actors disengage, replacing common purpose with pseudo-participation and compliance.

The engines of federal and state educational policy operate at a distance from daily life in schools, but in *Getting Schooled on Resistance* we nonetheless see their powerful shaping effect on the speed of trust. This is a story of life at Rosa Parks Middle School as teachers, administrators, and consultants take up a school improvement project, but it is also the story of life in an urban middle school under No Child Left Behind (NCLB) and its larger operational context of generalized, bureaucratized distrust. The teachers, students, consultants, and evaluators we meet are people of goodwill and intelligence, each in his or her way eager to make progress. But the key question—What does progress mean for the teachers and students of Rosa Parks Middle School?—is the one question they are not empowered to ask.

Stephen M. R. Covey, who coined the phrase "the speed of trust," saw trust as a professional, even economic variable. The architecture of trust includes more than personal integrity; it also encompasses performance. "Trust is a function of both character and competence," he has argued. "Of course you can't trust someone who lacks integrity, but hear this: If someone is honest but they can't perform . . . you won't trust them to get the job done" (Tonita, 2014). For many teachers, students, and administrators in U.S. schools, particularly for those serving the most challenged and marginalized communities, the particular mix of incentives, penalties, testing, and high-stakes accountability that characterized NCLB said very clearly: "We don't trust you to get the job done." Yet, as Cindy Urbanski argues, these are the only people who actually *can* get the job done.

For Covey, disengagement, bureaucracy, turnover, and churn were some of the "taxes" that deplete organizations where trust is low. But what if those same taxes create the conditions that produce low performance and continue to erode trust? How do parents, teachers, students, consultants, and researchers of goodwill and intelligence, such as those we meet at Rosa Parks Middle School, go forward to define and then make progress? We can only start by starting, and trusting in the possibility.

And perhaps we as a nation are getting ready as well. After years of false starts and delays, legislation to rewrite NCLB passed both houses of Congress and was signed into law by President Barack Obama on December 10, 2015. Responding to a growing consensus that NCLB's emphasis on standardized testing and high-stakes accountability, with its narrowing of curriculum, had gone too far, the new Every Student Succeeds Act emphasizes increased state and local responsibility and discretion in addressing accountability measures.

Whether this new policy context will help restore a sense of trust in education remains to be seen. For those who are schooled on resistance, the time to begin is now.

—Elyse Eidman-Aadah
Exectuive Director
National Writing Project
UC-Berkeley

REFERENCES

Covey, S. M. R., & Merrill, R. (2008). *The speed of trust: The one thing that changes everything*. New York, NY: Free Press.
Tonita, J. (2014, October 7). Working together at the speed of trust. *The Transformation Project* blog. Retrieved from stproject.org/general/working-together-at-the-speed-of-trust/

PREFACE

Untangling Urban Middle School Reform was first published in 2016. As I sit here working on the index for the new edition, which has reverted to the original title *Getting Schooled on Resistance,* I am reminded of what I already knew. The book is relevant and timely all these years later, and while the case study took place in a middle school, it is a book about K-12 schooling in the United States.

Getting Schooled is a book about resistance to the voices that say some students can't think critically due to their socioeconomic circumstances and the melatonin in their skin. It is a book about resistance to the "good" student and "bad" student monikers. In fact, it is a celebration of the "bad" student. It stands on the very shoulders of resistant thinkers. (Hello, Foucault!)

Getting Schooled is relevant in the post-pandemic K-12 classroom. While much has changed on the surface with the addition of chromebooks at every desk and remote learning days at the ready, the "programs" being trotted out are the same. They ask students for rote memorization. They ask students to do as they are told. They ask students to give back the exact information given to them. Teachers and students and even administrators who resist by thinking critically, and heaven forbid, outside of the box, are marked as "wrong" and "bad" and a "problem."

Getting Schooled is also relevant at the graduate level where things like Figured Worlds and Activity Theory and Critical Discourse Analysis are being taught as qualitative research methods. The book is a narrative of how such critical thinking about data can show society what is really at work when policy is made.

So why re-release a book about school reform from 2016 in 2024? Because. Resistance is always relevant.

PART I:

MAPPING CONFLICTING NARRATIVES

1:

INTRODUCING THE POWER IN STORY AND THE STORY OF POWER

Educational visionaries do not simply slot children into narrow roles
determined by those in power; they help children and society reinvent
our lives, generating structures that reflect our deepest values.

—Ayers and Ayers (2011) *Teaching the Taboo*, p. 19.

Urban schools is a curious term. It is often code for schools in city neighborhoods where the
poor and ethnic/racial minorities reside. It conjures images of a rectangular gray multistoried
building with small dirty windows secured behind a chain-link fence on black asphalt and
dirt. Other images might include dark halls with broken fluorescent lights and graffiti-
covered walls and police cars out front throwing blinking blue light onto the black and
brown faces of the students. One might imagine these students sitting sideways in the rows
of old desks with wobbly legs ignoring the teacher at the front of the room who is shouting
at them to quiet down and pay attention. The term evokes images of hard-faced adolescents
and others who have made their way into the building to sell drugs and weapons, dressed in
sagging pants and do-rags, chains hanging from their waists, or wearing revealing shirts and
tight jeans or short skirts. Perhaps they are fighting their way through the halls, banging into
the dented lockers and paying little mind to the clanging bells that direct them to the next
class, leaving trash and bloodshed in their wake. It is the term used to describe these hopeless
images of schooling in the inner cities of our country where one hero teacher—usually a
White woman, like Michelle Pfeiffer in *Dangerous Minds*, but maybe a Black man with a big
stick and a focus only on his work at school like Morgan Freeman in *Lean on Me*—comes in

and saves the students from themselves and all of the other callous educators in the building. This is the image of urban schools that persists in popular media and points toward the urban school reform story. By story, I mean the narrative in place that informs the actions and decisions made around urban school reform.

Outside of the movie theatres, Russakoff's (2015) book *The Prize* tells the story of Facebook founder Mark Zuckerberg's $100 million project to reform Newark, New Jersey's failing schools and create a national model of reform. Along with republican governor Chris Christie and democratic mayor Cory Booker, Zuckerberg and his wife dreamed of turning an entire school system around and creating a model that would do the same for the entire nation. The book unfolds as outsiders in the form of venture philanthropists, big politicians, and educational reform powerhouses with deficit views of teachers and students are critiqued by insiders. These insiders are on-the-ground grassroots teacher reformers, who plead for more community involvement in school reform decisions and more attention to students touched by extreme poverty and violence in community public schools as the answer to failing education, rather than charter schools. This too is the story of urban school reform; well-meaning, driven people caught up in a complex web of systemic issues of politics, poverty, and violence. This is another narrative that is both true and untrue.

In this book, I will bring forward the voices of the teachers and students of Rosa Parks Middle School (the name of the school and names of the consultants, teachers, administrators, and students are pseudonyms), voices that are often silenced in the urban school reform narrative. This book aims to tell some of their stories and to illustrate the complexity of negotiating multiple stories, especially when one story has more power than the others. In this book I want to look at the urban school reform story and the stories that intersect with it, particularly that of testing and accountability, and the teachers' and students' stories that call it into question. I want to tell the stories that are being silenced by the reform story. I will look deeply at the narratives that often work against the school reform story, a story that uses testing and accountability to shape educational programs to prove direct impact on student learning. I want to show how this fuller, richer understanding of what is happening in the school calls into question the restrictive framework that the focus on testing and accountability makes and the way testing and accountability is complicit in keeping people of poverty in their social position, also known as *social reproduction* (Bourdieu & Passeron 1990).

Rosa Parks Middle School was marked as low performing by the testing and accountability narrative, and that narrative determined the pedagogy by which the teachers were expected to teach. It fed into the restrictive framework mentioned above. This book will explore the ways in which the students at Rosa Parks Middle School were being socialized into this restrictive framework in ways that have the potential for social reproduction.

ROSA PARKS MIDDLE SCHOOL AND THE WRITING PROJECT

As National Writing Project consultants, I along with my colleagues Tallulah and Lauren were involved with Rosa Parks Middle School through a national grant we were awarded to help change the culture of writing in the school. Rosa Parks Middle School, serving grades six through eight, was built in 2005 after the district lost a federal case that eliminated school busing for desegregation and that, in effect, segregated the district's neighborhood schools. Prior to the case, neighborhood children had been bused over an hour to suburban schools. Rosa Parks is a public school that serves the neighborhood where it was built. In the local newspapers the neighborhood is considered a hub for gang activity. It is a place where city buses do not run on the streets after dark and where police sirens are reminders of the rape, murder, and larceny that occur there. In keeping with both reality and the urban school reform trope, the children needed a safe space to focus, a place to change direction, to turn around and to move out of the culture of violence that the school officials saw surrounding them.

The principals thought of the school as a beacon on the hill pointing to the right direction and a safe haven for the children and their families. The suburban school architecture of the building reflects that mission. The campus is on a well-kept expansive, grassy park that rises on a hill over the neighborhood, offering the students and their families an image of the success that education can bring. In Chapter 2 I will critique this beacon on a hill metaphor as playing into a deficit view of the neighborhood residents as well as the school's students. I will do so by pointing to the funds of knowledge the neighborhood people bring to the school through their own stories about how to be in the world, stories that are ignored and silenced by the dominant testing and accountability narrative that is so much a part of the urban school reform narrative.

The staff at Rosa Parks Middle School was quite transient. Many of the teachers were Teach for America educators, who by nature are only in the school for a short period of time. In the second year of the study, Dr. Carter, the first principal, left and Mrs. Morgan came, bringing an entirely new administration with her. The district also gave her the power to hire and fire teachers as she felt would best benefit the school and the students, so there was significant changeover during the final two years of the study.

The National Writing Project (NWP) is a federally funded program dedicated to professional development (PD) around the teaching of writing in kindergarten through college. Two major tenets of the program are a focus on teachers teaching teachers and teachers of writing being writers themselves. The program also has a strong basis in inquiry into teaching and learning, with an emphasis on teachers as researchers in their own classrooms. The program offers intensive summer institutes where teachers work together to delve deeply into theory and best practices around the teaching of writing and explore their own writing lives. The institute reflects the NWP's commitment to building trusting relationships with teachers so that they might think and work together. It also encourages the professionalization of teachers, as the institute is often for graduate school credit. Once teachers complete the institute, they are considered teacher consultants or TCs. These TCs then offer professional development in their own schools as well as schools that the local Writing Project serves. Tallulah and I are long-time TCs with backgrounds as teachers in urban schools and avid teacher researchers. Lauren is a university professor in English education and the director of our Writing Project site.

Rosa Parks Middle School became a part of an NWP national study of the effectiveness of NWP professional development because a principal who had worked with the Writing Project in a different school suggested that Rosa Parks Middle School participate in the study in order to improve its writing curriculum. We chose to work with Rosa Parks Middle School because we were interested in working in the context of the school. It was considered a low-performing school and we felt we could make a real difference there. At the time this choice was made the principal of Rosa Parks Middle School had no experience with the Writing Project and knew only that his mentor had told him it was a good idea to work with us.

The national study was a 3-year study in which the outside researchers collected quantitative and qualitative data in order to track improvement in student writing as a result of Writing Project professional development. The researchers collected writing samples throughout the course of the three years and interviewed teachers and administrators in the school as well as the consultants working in the school. They also collected narrative reports from the teachers and the consultants. I was in graduate school during the time of the study and decided to use the site to conduct my own research project around writing instruction in urban schools.

When we began our work in the school, the principal, Dr. Carter, assigned the academic facilitator and the head of the English department (the 7th-grade English teacher) to the project and told them to take care of what we needed. He was hands-off, particularly in the beginning. When we came to the school, writing instruction only happened in 7th-grade English/language arts (ELA) classrooms because that was the subject and grade level tested by the state. The 6th- and 8th-grade ELA classes were focused on reading. In the first year of the study, the state changed the writing test to incorporate science, math, and social studies content as well, so we began our work with a focus on writing across the curriculum.

In the second year of the study, a new principal, Mrs. Morgan, was hired, and she decided to adopt the Learning Focused School (LFS) curriculum outside of and in addition to the work being done with the Writing Project. LFS is a corporation that offers professional development and structure for teaching and learning. In addition to adopting LFS, the principal also adopted a computerized writing program, Achieve3000. Each day, the students received a nonfiction news item, written on their Lexile level (a measurement of a student's reading level), in an email. Students spent 45 minutes each day reading the article and taking notes on the computer when prompted. At the end they answered multiple-choice questions and then put their notes into the outline provided by the program in order to write an essay. The school was focused on the Common Core State Standards (CCSS) 8.1 for reading that emphasized picking out key details and connecting them back to the text. The computer program provided practice with this skill and experience with argumentative writing as well. The computer then scored the writing for the teachers, leaving them free to work with the other important things they needed to do for their students.

Mrs. Morgan assigned the assistant principal in charge of instruction to the Writing Project partnership. In the third year, through the assistant principal assigned to us, the school adopted an argument-only writing policy. According to the policy, students were only to write argumentative essays, no other types of essays and no poetry or fiction or anything else that may be considered creative writing. I will go into more detail about the narrow view of argumentation adopted by the school in Chapter 2.

Throughout the course of the study and our work with the school, Tallulah, Lauren, and I tried to work within the confines of these programs as best we could. Though the school considered the work with the Writing Project to be another program in addition to LFS, Achieve3000, and the argument-only writing policy, we worked hard to integrate our work into these programs and policies so that the students, teachers, and administrators could see how all of these things could work together rather than being separate items pulling them in different directions. This book will detail the ways in which we worked with these programs and policies.

Lauren asked Tallulah and me to lead the professional development at the school, and the three of us worked together on the project throughout the study. Tallulah and I were in the school at least once a month and then more frequently as time went on. We offered workshops on our site's college campus, after school at Rosa Parks, and during professional learning communities at Rosa Parks. We began with a focus on teachers as writers and then moved to writing for the standardized test in a process-oriented way once the teachers requested that we focus our PD in that area. When Learning Focused Schools was adopted and emphasized the idea of rigor even more, we offered workshops on reimagining rigor and the writing process and then on ways of re-seeing argument as the argument-only policy and Achieve3000 were adopted.

As we worked with the teachers, we spent more and more time with subjects other than ELA because of the new requirements to get writing into all courses. Also, the other content area teachers felt they had more room to experiment because writing time in ELA was totally taken up by Achieve3000. As I developed my own teacher research, I became particularly interested in what was happening in two social studies teachers' classrooms. In the second year of the study, there was a moment when a 6th-grade social studies teacher tried out an activity we had shared about multigenre writing. Samuel's story and the stories of his students are told in Chapters 4, 5, and 6. In the third year of the study, a 7th-grade social studies teacher became very interested in daybooks, one of the tools we introduced to the teachers for process writing (I will go into more details about daybooks later). As a result of his interest, I chose his class as a site for my own study of writing in this school. I visited Ronald and his students once a week for a semester. I interviewed his students and collected samples of their writing. I also observed classes and taught model lessons. Ronald's story and the stories of his students are also told in Chapters 4, 5, and 6.

URBAN SCHOOL REFORM, TESTING, AND ACCOUNTABILITY

This dominant narrative of the urban school that Rosa Parks Middle School is a part of is also a part of the wider educational reform story in the United States and has unfolded over many years. In 1981, Secretary of Education T. H. Bell under President Ronald Reagan appointed a National Commission on Excellence in Education in order to look closely at America's schooling. The result was a report titled *A Nation at Risk* that used bold and urgent language to describe what it called the mediocre state of schools in the United States and argued for states to adopt "tougher standards, stronger graduation requirements, more rigorous curriculum, better pay for teachers and improved teacher training" (Hess & Petrilli, 2007, p. 11). This report put education reform on the map for many Americans and made it a central issue in elections.

Leadership from the nation's "Education Governors," one of which was then Governor Bill Clinton of Arkansas, proved that the education reform story was a bipartisan movement. As leader of the National Governor's Association, Clinton supported the ideas in *A Nation at Risk* and urged states to raise their standards in education. In 1994, during Clinton's presidency, the Elementary and Secondary Education Act came up for reauthorization. The reauthorized law required that all states create performance-based accountability systems for schools by the year 2000 (Hess & Petrilli, 2007). Though most states failed to comply, the story of urban school reform was starting to take shape with the testing and accountability narrative firmly affixed.

In 2001 No Child Left Behind (NCLB) was written into law under George W. Bush with proud support from leaders in both the republican and democratic parties. Republican Joe Boehner called the bill his "proudest achievement" while in office, and democrat Ted Kennedy said, "This is a defining issue about the future of our nation and about the future of democracy, the future of liberty, and the future of the United States in leading the free world. No piece of legislation will have a greater impact or influence on that" (Hess & Petrilli, 2007, p. 4).

The story of urban school reform told by NCLB was that all students in the United States deserved a fair shake. This bill had massive bipartisan support. In each instance, the battle cry was for raising the standards for education and turning around low performing schools, most often found in inner-city urban settings, in order to raise test scores. In their interpretation of the bill, states began to link teacher pay to standardized testing. Schools where students were not increasing their test scores were taken over by the state, and outsiders were sent in in order to fix what was seen as broken.

As the urban education reform story continued to unfold in the Obama administration, a beltway group devised a set of national standards in math and English/language arts, funded largely by various corporate foundations and with hurried consultation with professional organizations. At the same time, Secretary of Education Arne Duncan launched Race to the Top, an initiative that consolidated block grants that used to go to individual states and made these funds competitive between the states. In order to be considered for Race to the Top dollars, state education officials felt as though they would be more competitive if they adopted College and Career Readiness Standards. States that adopted the College and Career Readiness Standards, which later became the Common Core State Standards (CCSS), would measure student learning using common federally developed assessments. For the first time in the nation's history, states would not have the responsibility for setting goals for student learning or deciding if statewide testing would provide the benchmarks for student learning. Almost immediately after the CCSS were widely adopted, states started to opt out of these programs.

These seemingly shared aims of the Common Core are described in the mission statement of the group who developed them:

> The Common Core State Standards provide a consistent, clear understanding of what students are expected to learn, so teachers and parents know what they need to do to help them. The standards are designed to be robust and relevant to the real world, reflecting the knowledge and skills that our young people need for success in college and careers. With American students fully prepared for the

future, our communities will be best positioned to compete successfully in the global economy.

This book tells the story of one urban school, Rosa Parks Middle School, in a Race to the Top state where learning is a daily struggle and where teachers and children are considered low performing. Rosa Parks Middle School is the kind of school that the CCSS was designed to help. But *helping* is a problematic term. This story explores how "a consistent, clear understanding of what students are expected to learn" becomes opaque within instrumentalist operations—the drill and skill of the testing and accountability narrative—that makes learning for these children problematic. This story describes how the "robust" and "relevant" standards designed for the "real world" touted in the quote above actually construct a fairy-tale world where the costumes of school uniforms can't quite create the illusion of success, and how the mechanization—the tracking and scoring of learning—creates the smoke and mirrors of progress, or the lack thereof. This story describes how America's poor are being positioned and prepared for the future. It is a story of social reproduction where marginalized populations are kept on the margins by the system that is meant to provide them with social mobility.

The story of educational reform, particularly the story of urban school reform, while intending to create fair and equitable education for all students in the United States, views the students, teachers, and administrators of Rosa Parks Middle School through a deficit lens, as people incapable of doing, or simply not caring enough to do, the hard work of teaching and learning that is required to pass the tests. The story also proposes that outsiders come in to turn the failing school around, playing into the deficit model by suggesting once again that the people in the school don't have what it takes to be "successful" on their own.

REFRAMING THE STORY AND FRAMING THE BOOK

The descriptive image at the opening of this chapter is one story of urban schools, but there are other stories about urban schools that have not yet captured the popular imagination. The problem with the dominant narrative of the urban school story is that it has become a single story. In her TED Talk, "The Danger of a Single Story," Chimamanda Ngozi Adichie (2013) says, "The single story creates stereotypes, and the problem with stereotypes is not that they are untrue, but that they are incomplete. They make one story become the only story." A single story has power, the power to construct and influence the world of a person or group of people.

The multiple stories circulating in the school—stories of democratizing education, measuring growth and development, and learning to read and write—are all part of the larger story of urban school reform. These are all stories that the students, teachers, administrators, and consultants must negotiate. The dominant story (not necessarily true) is that Rosa Parks Middle School is a troubled school, and the insiders there (teachers and students) need to be changed by outsiders brought in to improve the culture of the school, a culture of failure brought about by inadequate teaching and troubled and unfocused poor children.

The competing and conflicting narratives in the school construct not only who has power and who does not in the world of the school, but also what it means to be in this world. And as the participants negotiated these competing narratives of which way they should turn and what they move toward, they were caught in a figurative pinball game that seemed to me to be never ending.

Both principals were charged by the district leadership to bring order to the school and to bring up the test scores. The second principal, Mrs. Morgan, was given the power to strategically staff the school—to remove those teachers who had not performed or could not perform well with these children and to bring in those who could. Both principals mandated that teachers follow the district pacing guide, a guide detailing what was to be taught and when throughout the district, and that teachers use scripted lessons to challenge the students and help them prepare for common district-mandated quarterly tests and high-stakes end-of-grade tests held in May. To the principals, the pacing guides and scripted lessons represented the correct direction.

At the same time, the Writing Project consultants, Tallulah, Lauren, and I, were trying to control the curriculum so that writing could happen in this same world and we could prove the effectiveness of professional development and our methods of democratizing education. We saw the principals' pursuit of order and control as seriously limiting teacher leadership and professionalism and student engagement. In our view, the principals had the school heading in the wrong direction. In fact, we wanted everyone to turn around and go our way of integrating writing into all aspects of thinking and learning. Chapter 2 will examine these two competing narratives in detail in order to illuminate what the teachers and students, administrators and consultants were negotiating in the school. Chapter 3 makes use of *activity theory* in order to set Rosa Parks Middle School into the context of the urban school reform story. We will examine school uniforms and teaching methods in the school and the way the dominant narrative initiates social reproduction while the modicum of agency possessed by the teachers and students creates, through acts of resistance, the possibility for social change.

These chapters make up Part I of this book, which is concerned with setting Rosa Parks Middle School within the larger context of urban school reform in the United States.

Part II of the book narrows the lens to look specifically at what it means to be teachers and students of writing in Rosa Parks Middle School. Chapter 4 takes a look at two social studies teachers who took varying degrees of interest in what we were offering in professional development. One took an assignment offered in the workshop and worked in compliance with both the consultants and the administrators to carry out that assignment in his classroom. The other resisted the school's argument-only policy in order to fully adopt our daybook strategy. In essence, Chapter 4 is a story of the negotiation of resistance and compliance with the competing narratives of the consultants and the principals on the part of these two teachers. Chapter 5 looks at three students who are compliant and shows the way in which social reproduction is operating on them through their writing. Chapter 6 focuses on one resistant student and the opportunity for change and social mobility that her resistance through writing implies.

Chapter 7 is a conclusion and sums up the story of our (the consultants) work in the school and what happened there from our vantage point. It broadens the lens once more in order to call for a critique of the testing and accountability narrative found in the urban school reform narrative. It focuses on the resistance and compliance of teachers and students as a critique of the narratives that keep students trapped in poverty and teachers following scripts. The chapter offers discussion points for teachers and administrators who wish to illuminate the competing and conflicting narratives they and their students are negotiating and to inquire how to critique the power narratives in ways that have positive material results for students and schools.

2:

ROSA PARKS MIDDLE SCHOOL

CONTRASTING AND CONFLICTING STORIES

The first day that Tallulah, Lauren, and I drove down the fairy-tale named streets lined by single-family homes cramped next to one another on our way to Rosa Parks Middle School, the irony did not escape us. The boarded-up houses and those remaining with bars on windows and overgrown yards were no fairytale castles, and we certainly didn't imagine ourselves as Prince Charming, charging on the scene to save the day. In fact, we were hoping to drive by unnoticed. The school appeared to be walled off from the rest of the community. We had to enter the property through a gate that was locked after hours, and Tallulah commented on the fence surrounding the property. A police car was parked in the drive near the entryway. The school seemed out of place, appearing to mock the people who lived around the school in its position towering over them. It looked to me like the school I'd been working in the week before in an affluent neighborhood.

As PhD students, Tallulah and I had been reading a lot of Foucault, and our initial views of the school were seen through that lens. Everywhere we looked we saw people working very hard on behalf of the children in the community, a community whose fairytale street names attempted to mask the poverty and neglect of the people living there. The school, rising above the community like Sleeping Beauty's castle on an expansive grassy hill, was in deep contrast to the architecture in the valley below, where small single-family homes were built on tiny, cramped lots with overgrown yards and beat up furniture on the front porches.

Inside, the school looked like Foucault's *panopticon*, a building where a single watchman can keep an eye on all that is happening at the same time. The structure was built in such as way as to allow the administrators to stand in a central location and see down each hall. For Tallulah, Lauren, and me, there was an antiseptic feel to the school inside. The walls were sterile and the absence of student work was unwelcoming. Motivational posters were hanging on the walls, including the iconic one with a cat holding on to a pole and the inscription "Hang in there." There was also one with a pink horse in full canter, mane and tale floating, and the words, "If you can dream it, you can achieve it." This stoic place did not look like it would welcome frivolity like pink horse riding and kitten shenanigans in the halls! But there was something even more troubling here. The posters—like the cat ready to fall in "Hang in there"—engendered the idea of students hanging on by just their grips, not standing on solid ground. The horse, holding out an image of "a dream," while echoing Dr. King's famous speech, had a potentially dual meaning in which any student who fails to achieve is blamed for failing to dream hard enough.

Our response to the school inside and out informed our initial story of the school. It was a narrative that we were creating and assigning to the school. But our story of the school was not the only one. In this chapter I look closely at the multiple stories of the school, using the theory of figured worlds and sociohistorical theories of language to see the ways in which these stories construct the material reality of the world we live in. I also examine the idea of social reproduction to introduce the way in which the power narrative is solidifying the students' social position. From there I look at just two competing stories of Rosa Parks Middle School—that of the consultants (my colleagues and I), and that of the administrators—in order to illustrate some of the competing ways of being that the students and teachers had to negotiate. Both the consultants and the administrators were trying to get the teachers to move in a certain direction, according to their narrative and construction of knowledge, and both had great intentions. Teachers and students were thus forced to exist in both narratives (as well as others illustrated later in the book) as they tried to negotiate the right path toward knowledge and success. In the rest of the chapter, I look specifically at the structures in place in the school for students and teachers, and how they learn and teach writing through the competing narratives of the consultants and the school principals.

FIGURING THE STORY

Holland, Lachicotte, Skinner, and Cain (1998) describe social relations as being constructed in *figured worlds*, "socially and culturally constructed realm[s] of interpretation in which particular characters and actors are recognized, significance is assigned to certain acts, and particular outcomes are valued over others" (p. 52). They describe these figured worlds as *narrativized*. "Narrativized . . . convey[s] the idea that many of the elements of a world relate to one another in the form of a story . . . a 'standard plot' against which narratives of unusual events are told" (p. 53). These narratives are not prescriptive, but are "significant as a backdrop for interpretation" (p. 54). At Rosa Parks Middle School, the testing and accountability narrative of what counts as knowledge is then a part of the standard plot of the school. Some of the narratives working within or against that standard plot were the Writing Project's narrative of what counts as knowledge and the narratives of the teachers and students in the building who were also trying to figure out how to perform their school identities. The testing and accountability narrative had more institutional power than any of these other narratives, and from this position the institution of testing and accountability was able to name and choose what knowledge counts, which has the material result of focusing the administrators and teachers on test scores, thus marginalizing the other narratives working in and through the school.

There is much at stake in the narratives evoked by the term *urban schools* and the material realities—the competing, conflicting, and counter narratives—that work within and against the normalizing narratives of our culture. At Rosa Parks Middle School, they animated each other in a struggle for what Foucault (1980) describes as the naming of this world, its participants, the rituals of schooling, and the concepts such as order, control, and responsibility that circulated there. His term for this act of naming is *Truth claims*—forms of power/knowledge that inscribe and produce how the participants in a figured world see one another and, in the world of schooling, an understanding of how children learn and what role literacy has in that learning. Truth claims produce the official discourses of schooling and urban reform and are the normalizing storylines by which people understand what happens in the school and how to be there. In this way the competing narratives and normalizing storylines of the participants in the school construct the world of Rosa Parks Middle School and legitimize the institution of schooling.

Sociohistorical theories of discourse and language (e.g., Foucault, 1980, and Bakhtin, 1981) explain that there are multiple narratives, or socially and historically constructed *regimes of truth* (Foucault, 1980), that are constantly operating in and through people that produce their understanding about how to act in a particular world as it is constructed. Holland et al.'s (1998) argument that people participate in multiple figured worlds denotes the social and historical construction of these "realms of interpretation" (p. 52). The school participants, then, have narratives from multiple figured worlds in addition to the ones of the school world that are operating on them and are in dialogue with, in conflict with, or counter to the narratives of urban school reform, which are also working on, in, and through them. All of those narratives are in a constant struggle for hegemony and are thus constantly forming each participant's storyline of how to be a teacher, administrator, consultant, or student in the figured world of Rosa Parks Middle School.

These competing and conflicting narratives make urban school reform incredibly complex for all those involved in it and explain why common-sense solutions like testing and accountability measures are failing to bring the reform they seek. They are instead becoming complicit in the phenomena of social reproduction. Sociologists Bourdieu and Passeron (1990) argue that the school world works to reproduce dominant ideology. Bourdieu and Passeron also point out that the dominant ideology is arbitrary and socially constructed. School ways of knowing and being are created by the dominant group and thereby reflect and legitimize the ways of being in the world of that group. The socialization process is a part of the "hidden curriculum" of schools described by critical theorist and education researcher Henry Giroux (1983). Foucault (1977) names the school as one of the great "normalizing" institutions of what he calls the carceral society. He believed that these institutions actually produce delinquency. Student discourse that does not "fit" into or disrupts the socialization process of school marks that student as deficient and delinquent. In Foucault's view this phenomenon of social reproduction acts as a training ground for prison in that students are seen as delinquent and limited in their freedom to move about the building, talk with one another, express themselves through dress, and even think for themselves because of the ways in which they may disrupt the socialization process of school. The idea of a school as a training ground for prison is an extreme one; however, it rang true for us (the consultants) as we experienced the strict rules of Rosa Parks Middle School. But again, this is just one story of the school in multiple stories that will be represented.

Below, I will illustrate my narrative and that of my colleagues as Writing Project teacher consultants alongside that of the school administrators in order to look closely at the idea of the competing narratives that teachers and students must negotiate in the school. These are but two of the narratives being negotiated; however, I have chosen them because they are emblematic of the well-meaning, hardworking people involved and the power of the testing and accountability narrative over other narratives.

ROSA PARKS MIDDLE SCHOOL FROM OUR OUTSIDER/CONSULTANT PERSPECTIVE

Tallulah, Lauren, and I came to Rosa Parks Middle School eager and excited about the possibilities of working with urban middle school teachers and their students. Tallulah and I had both taught for years in urban schools, so going into this project we felt that we would be among familiar colleagues and that we could work together to engage their students as learners and writers. We anticipated that the school's teachers would be a large group of colleagues with which we could talk to face to face. We wanted to turn around the corner-facing isolation we had felt in our own buildings where we often found ourselves alone in our approaches to literacy instruction. We wanted to turn the teachers toward the kinds of conversations we often had via Skype with one another and our other Writing Project colleagues after hours, to think together about the work that we had been doing behind our closed doors. In our view, a building full of teachers working openly together to think about engaging children in writing in transformative ways was the right direction to be heading.

Tallulah, Lauren, and I had been thinking deeply about the importance of *dialogic teaching*—using the power of talk between students and teachers in dialogue to enhance learning—and constructing our classrooms around that idea in our conversations in our graduate program as well as our conversations in our Writing Project Site. We were working to turn away from banking concepts of teaching and learning (Freire, 1997), in which the instructor deposits the knowledge into the students, and toward a concept that recognized that both teacher and student have important knowledge to share and that both would learn by sharing that knowledge through equal dialogue with one another (Freire, 1997). Dialogic teaching also fit with our Writing Project sites' understanding of the National Writing Project principle of teachers teaching teachers. Tallulah, Lauren, and I had knowledge to share in this school as teachers, and so did the teachers there. We saw our professional development work as a dialogue, an exchange of ideas where we all learned from one another, sharing our expertise together as colleagues interested in students' writing, thinking, and learning.

However, our work at Rosa Parks Middle School was different from any Writing Project work we had engaged in before. As noted in Chapter 1, our site was part of a federal national study evaluating the efficacy of Writing Project professional development. Typically, NWP develops a relationship with teachers in a school over time, and our partner schools do not require teachers to participate in our professional development. Rather, teachers who attend our workshops come voluntarily. We had no prior relationship with Rosa Parks Middle School, so we had to begin a partnership from scratch. We did spend time getting to know teachers and trying to create a common culture that centered in writing instruction to share with them; however, we were aware of the complexity of our Writing Project being studied in a school where teacher turnover and administrative changes were constant. Another big difference was that during the first year, working with us was compulsory for the teachers, rather than voluntary as we were accustomed to. Finally, we usually begin a partnership with a school because some of its teachers have attended our four-week intensive Summer Institute and are excited about sharing what they learned with their colleagues. At Rosa Parks Middle School, only one teacher was ever able to attend our Summer Institute. Writing Project professional development is built on the foundation of deep, trusting relationships and a strong understanding of the current research on writing instruction. We didn't have those relationships at Rosa Parks Middle School, and it was difficult to build them along with the strong research base when teachers were unable to attend our intensive institute and were moving in and out of the building.

In Rosa Parks Middle School we were outsiders, and our ways of being in the figured world of the school and our reasons for being there marked us as such. Our email conversations with each other were often about being misunderstood or ignored, or how we saw things differently from the school's point of view. It wasn't just the visitor's sticker or the escort that took us to the classrooms we were visiting that marked us. It wasn't even the conversations in the lounge where we explained again and again that we were not there as state inspectors but as teachers and colleagues interested in thinking with other teachers about writing and learning in the school, as the teachers packed up their lunches from the microwave and went to eat together somewhere where we were not. Our outsider status was even deeper than that. To the teachers, the direction we were asking them to turn and the destination to which we were asking them to go seemed impossible. The empty composition notebooks we gave them to fill with writing were just another burden, another thing they had to do, another thing miring them in place.

STRUCTURES FOR STUDENTS

Tallulah, Lauren, and I were startled by the operations of the school on our first visit. As I mentioned before, due to our work with Foucault as a part of our PhD program, we saw everything through the power/knowledge lens, where power is everywhere all the time and all knowledge and truth is an effect of that power. Power and knowledge are integrally related and produce social positioning. (Kamberelis & Dimitriadis, 2005). We saw middle school students moving through the halls with their hands behind their backs like prison inmates as teachers spoke to them through bullhorns like prison guards. We saw students dressed in ways that conflicted with the rich cultures of their home lives. We saw panopticon-like surveillance, where students were not trusted to go to the restroom without strict adult supervision and had no space to talk with each other as silence was demanded in classrooms, in the hallways, and in the cafeteria. We saw students who were not trusted to take the school's books from the classroom or use the lockers to store them so that they might study at home. In classes, we saw students regurgitating textbook information poured into them as if they were empty vessels with no thoughts and ideas of their own. This regurgitation took the form of rote memorization, worksheets, and formulaic writing practices that smacked of worksheets. Even the class notes were fill-in-the-blank worksheets.

STRUCTURES FOR TEACHERS AND CONSULTANTS

In an effort to work with the teachers' overloaded schedules, Tallulah, Lauren, and I devised a plan to work individually with teachers during their planning periods and during scheduled content meetings. We were hoping to make use of already scheduled meeting time but turn it toward what we saw as a more productive direction. We worked to familiarize ourselves with the ever-changing meeting schedules of the school and find a way to work within them. Our scheduled plans were bumped often, however, by everything from teams sent in by the state to intervene in the school because of low test scores, to Personal Education Plan documentation, in which teachers had to detail an intervention plan specific to each student in the school. (This is different from an individualized education plan because no disability has to be proven.) These interruptions took precedence over our plans because the academic facilitator and teacher leader placed in charge of the NWP program did not have the power to protect the time we had set apart for workshops from administrators' initiatives.

And yet, there were teachers who found a way to turn in our direction. As people got to know Tallulah, Lauren, and I through the workshops we offered and the meetings we attended, some teachers (although certainly not all of them) began to see us as being on their side. We began to see that some of our most fruitful conversations happened in the hall, when teachers heard that we were in the building and came out of classrooms to stop us and ask a question, or pulled us in to show us this "cool writing thing" the students were doing, or when we went to lunch with the teachers and their students. We felt like these conversations were productive and valuable, but we constantly struggled with feeling that the time was inefficiently spent as the careful, orderly plans we made for workshops and meetings were pushed aside and we were only able to really work with the teachers one-on-one, which was not our ideal. We wanted to turn the whole school around, and in that desire, no matter how well intentioned, we were working within the dominant deficit narrative of urban school reform.

STRUCTURES FOR WRITING

When the research team conducting the national evaluation study of the NWP visited the school for the first time, they contacted us and asked if we were sure that we wanted to be in this school. They had seen almost no writing while they were there. They were concerned that they had seen only the highly formulaic writing test practice that was happening in the 7th-grade ELA classes. They understood the Writing Project's culture of writing instruction to include all subjects and grade levels in a process-oriented constructivist approach that was extremely different from what they were seeing, and they worried that the mismatch would be too great of a challenge to overcome. In our own initial visit, we saw narrow practices of teaching, particularly in writing, that required students to regurgitate the information given to them by the teacher, to fill in blanks, that left almost no space for critical thinking. We said to ourselves, "it's no wonder the students 'don't write!'"

We were eager to turn the formulaic notions of writing in a direction that connected students' daily lives with school subjects and to work with students and teachers to use writing as a way to inquire into legitimizing power structures that we saw as marginalizing the students and staff. We were thrilled to have three years to think deeply with teachers about what was happening in their classrooms and about ways in which to bring a culture of writing to the school.

We started our work with the teachers by inviting them to a writing retreat on our NWP site's university campus before school started. We wanted the teachers to be able to attend our four-week Summer Institute, but that was impossible because of their summer jobs and child care concerns. Knowing we needed a saturated period of time to build relationships and begin to delve into current research around writing instruction, we created a retreat that met on Thursday evening, Friday, and Saturday, requiring less time away from jobs and family.

At the time, the irony of getting the teachers out of Rosa Parks Middle School and turning them toward yet another castle on the hill *did* escape us. We were holding the university up as a place with all the answers. At the retreat, the teachers worked together as a team and wrote individually in daybooks to collect their thoughts. *Daybooks* (Brannon, Griffin, Haag, Iannone, Urbanski, & Woodward, 2008) are essentially writer's notebooks, but they are also more than that. They are a place to think on the page, a place to be messy and get the ideas swirling in the mind recorded so that they might be worked with later, and also a place to collect handouts, research, and other snippets of information. They take the place of the typical school binder and worksheets and instead invite creative, critical thinking and writing.

We shared several activities that we use to get students writing in daybooks and had the teachers experience these activities for themselves. Table 2.1 lists some of these activities. The idea behind all of them is to get both teachers and students thinking like writers, people who put their ideas down on paper and then play with them to form longer pieces of writing. This was a direct contrast to the fill-in-the-blank approach we were seeing in the school.

Our plan was to give the teachers a space to be writers. The teachers appeared excited by the experience, and we thought that this would translate quickly to their work in the classroom, work that we felt they were not doing and needed to do, like teaching writing and making space for students to think their own thoughts through writing. But when we went to the school a few weeks after the retreat to check in with the teachers, it was almost

TABLE 2.1. DAYBOOK WRITING ACTIVITIES

Writing Tool	Purpose of Tool	Instructions
Writing into the Day	To focus students on the topic of instruction for the day	Freewrite a response to a teacher-developed prompt, detailing all you know about it and what you are thinking about what you know.
Quick Write	To get thoughts down on paper	When students are having a lively discussion about a topic in the course, stop them and ask them to write for five minutes to capture what's on their minds and what is happening in the discussion.
Double Entry Journal (Bertoff, 1981)	To get students pointing to the text and thinking about it	Create 2 columns in daybook. Column 1 is a quote, summary question, or note about the text. Column 2 is the student's written response to Column 1.
Dialectic Journal (Urbanski, 2006)	To get students pointing to the text and discussing it with each other in writing	Create 4 columns in daybook. Column 1 is a quote, summary, question, or note about the text. Column 2 is the student's written response to Column 1. Column 3 is a partner's response to Columns 1 & 2. Column 4 is the original student's thoughts on what they are thinking now based on the written discussion.
Summary, Response, Connection	To get students responding to and thinking about text through writing and connecting that text with lived experience and things they already know about	The student first writes a summary of the text (reading, discussion, PowerPoint, video, etc.). The student then writes a personal response to that summary connecting it up with their own thinking. Finally, the student connects the text to something in their lives. This can be as narrow as text-to-self and as broad as text-to-world.

as if the writing we did never happened. Nothing in the teachers' practices had changed. The writing didn't materialize in their classrooms because the retreat did not map onto the teachers' school world. Seeing the mismatch between the teachers' realities and the direction we had offered in the summer, Tallulah and I began to observe classes, teach model lessons during classes, and meet with teachers during their planning periods in an attempt to walk in their shoes as teachers in the world of Rosa Parks Middle School. We saw formulaic five-paragraph essays being assigned in order to meet what the teachers and administrators saw as the requirements of the state test. Tallulah and I tried to convince the teachers that writing in forms other than the five-paragraph essay could engender careful, critical thinking on the part of the writer and in many ways required much more critical thinking than the formulaic, fill-in-the-blank essay assignment did, while at the same time engaging students much more deeply. We met stony-faced and very vocal resistance.

In one workshop, we offered the idea of teaching argument through forms of writing such as letters, blog posts, and poetry. One teacher became visibly upset, pushing his chair back away from the group and refusing to participate in what we were doing. When it came time for discussion, he exploded. "You don't think our students are smart enough to write real essays. You are asking us to give them assignments that are for elementary school children and will not prepare them for high school and college. This is ridiculous." The teachers in the room nodded along with him, and in their reflections for the day they all said something along the lines of "this is not good enough for our students." For them, real school writing did not include forms such as letters, blog posts, and poetry. In their view, our suggestions led off the road of academic achievement toward a playground meant only for students who were incapable of writing essays. They felt that Tallulah, Lauren, and I were merely appeasing and entertaining the students, rather than preparing them for the rigors of higher education, and in that way, suggesting that the students were simply stuck in their current lives of poverty and violence. Tallulah, Lauren, and I had the same goals for the students as the teachers and staff did; however, we all vehemently disagreed on how to get there. Rather than being in dialogue about how to best serve the students through writing instruction, we were standing in the middle of the road arguing over which map was right.

When the writing practices of the school narrowed even further in our third year there with the argument-only policy and the adoption of Achieve3000, Tallulah, Lauren, and I cringed, took a deep breath, and then continued to push the teachers in the direction of *our* conception of writing instruction. In hindsight, we were treating the teachers as passive when they had proven to us that they were anything but. We offered a nuanced definition of argument that included many forms of argumentative writing as a counter to the five-paragraph argument structure that the new assistant administrator in charge of instruction insisted on. We offered a series of workshops on rigorous writing in order to put our definition of argument and rigor on the map of the school.

By this time in our work with Rosa Parks Middle School, we had planned every workshop very carefully, narrating for each other exactly what we would say. Lauren, Tallulah, and I wrote out narratives along with our agendas in order to check in with each other, working to ensure that we were connecting up our thinking with the needs of the school. Below is a narrative agenda for the rigorous writing workshop. Italics represent what we planned to say. Regular font is the actual agenda that the teachers saw.

(RE)IMAGINING RIGOR IN WRITING

Narrative: *I have attempted to plan this workshop using as many of the 10 Rosa Parks Middle School "must haves" as I could. This is an attempt to show how this stuff that we've been working on together over the past few years in terms of writing and learning fits in quite nicely with the Learning-Focused Schools initiative. I invite you all to let me know how I'm doing. Also, please be conscious of the texts and activities we are engaging in as we think together about these concepts. My hope is that you will find some tools for your classrooms here.*

3:45–4:00 Writing into the Workshop (Launch Activity)

Think about a time when you found yourself engaged in "rigorous" writing. What was the purpose of the writing? What made it "rigorous?" What made it engaging? (7 min.)

Share responses/Work together from responses to create a definition of "rigor."

Narrative: *Over the past few years, we've been looking really carefully into writing to learn in all content areas. We've talked about daybooks as a place for students to create small bits of writing as they process content area information, and as a place for them to explore ideas and try out ways of writing. What we want to do now is take all of that to the next level. We want to begin thinking about ways to use all of those small bits of writing that you all are incorporating into your classrooms to build larger pieces of writing. Today, we want to focus specifically on what "text" means in different content areas, and then look at how the small bits of writing and daily reading of those texts can lead up to and support a larger piece of writing.*

Let's begin with a non-traditional "text" about, well, text. We are going to listen to a three-minute excerpt from a podcast given by Elizabeth Moje. She is speaking about a concern that many of the content-area teachers here at Rosa Parks Middle School have raised in terms of "literacy" or "writing" instruction taking away time for students to engage in the ideas of the subject matter in the content areas. Moje is agreeing with that and challenging us to re-envision our ideas of "text." In this excerpt she is imagining what a classroom engaged with this re-envisioned idea of text might look like.

4:00–4:30 Content Specific "Writing"/ Double Entry Journals/ Cornell Notes

Create two columns in your daybook. In the Writing Project we refer to this activity as a Double Entry Journal, but many of you have said that it resembles the Cornell Notes you are already using.

- Listen to the Moje podcast about text (3 min.). While you are listening, jot down key ideas that jump out for you in Column 1.
- Take 3 minutes to write about what you are thinking here.
- In small groups, discuss the piece—get the "center" of gravity for your group.

- Make a list of "texts" for your content area (interactive vocabulary).
- Put the center of gravity and "texts" list on a big sticky note.
- Share with the whole group.

Narrative: *From here, we want to start crafting some writing assignments that engage students in the production of the texts they are exploring and learning about. We can think of the texts we are exploring in class as "mentor texts" for what the students will be composing. We also want to think about how we can intentionally craft our small, quick writes/writing-to-learn activities over the course of a unit to scaffold and build information, ideas, and concepts that students can mine for their larger writing projects.*

4:30–5:05 Rigorous Writing Assignments
- Individuals work on Rigorous Writing Assignments activity in content area groups (10 min.)
- Volunteers share concepts with the large group. Work together as a large group to "write" a model writing assignment based on the concepts (10 min).
- Small groups create writing assignments (15 min.)

5:05–5:15 Reflections and Homework
Writing Out of the Session . . . What "Learning Focused Schools/Rosa Parks Middle School Must-Haves" did you notice in the workshop—and more importantly, how do you see this material fitting into what you are doing in your classroom with learning focused schools? What are you thinking now about "rigorous writing" and "text" and how you might use those concepts to support knowledge-making in your content area?

Homework Narrative: *Over the next month or so, try this out. Use and tweak the assignment that you've created here along with the small bits of daily writing you've used to scaffold that assignment. Let students know that the small bits are building the large assignments and give them some class time to mine those small bits for a draft of the large assignment.*
- *Please bring samples of your assignments, the small writings that lead up to it, and students' writing to our next meeting. We can all look at these together and problem-solve. We will also talk about how to respond to these "rigorous" writing assignments in a way that keeps students writing and pushes them forward.*
- *Feel free to email any questions or sample assignments to Tallulah and me.*

Figure 2.1 shows a learning map we created that incorporates the structure and vocabulary of the Learning Focused Schools curriculum, which the school had adopted, to illustrate and connect up the ideas about rigor and writing that we were discussing in the workshop. Figure 2.2 shows the activity we asked teachers to complete in the first workshop in the series. These show our attempt to merge all of the work we had been doing with the daybook into the "new" curriculum and illustrate how the idea of rigorous writing assignments could be used in all subject areas.

FIGURE 2.1. (RE)IMAGINING RIGOROUS WRITING WITH LEARNING FOCUSED SCHOOLS

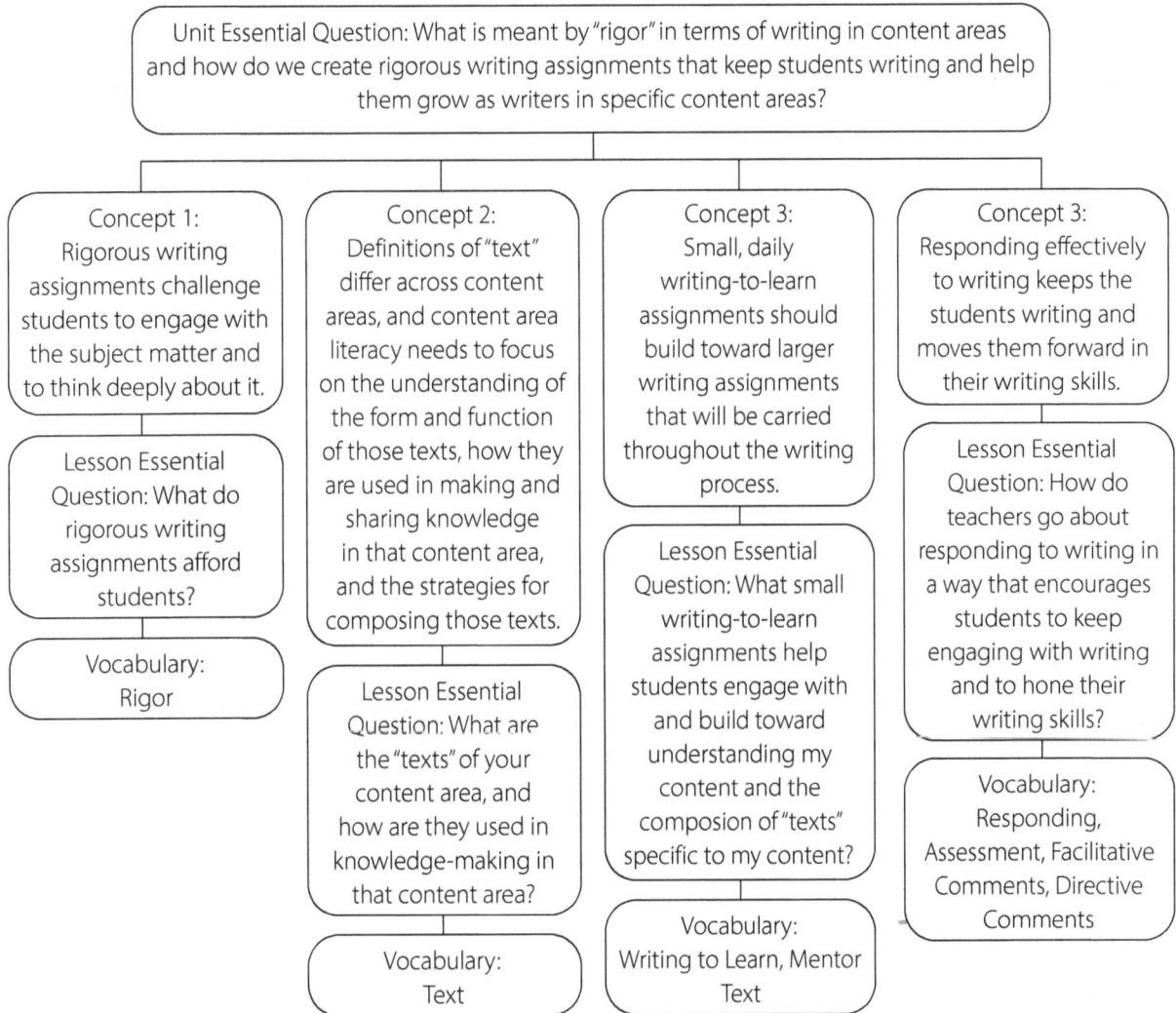

Unit Essential Question: What is meant by "rigor" in terms of writing in content areas and how do we create rigorous writing assignments that keep students writing and help them grow as writers in specific content areas?

Concept 1: Rigorous writing assignments challenge students to engage with the subject matter and to think deeply about it.

Lesson Essential Question: What do rigorous writing assignments afford students?

Vocabulary: Rigor

Concept 2: Definitions of "text" differ across content areas, and content area literacy needs to focus on the understanding of the form and function of those texts, how they are used in making and sharing knowledge in that content area, and the strategies for composing those texts.

Lesson Essential Question: What are the "texts" of your content area, and how are they used in knowledge-making in that content area?

Vocabulary: Text

Concept 3: Small, daily writing-to-learn assignments should build toward larger writing assignments that will be carried throughout the writing process.

Lesson Essential Question: What small writing-to-learn assignments help students engage with and build toward understanding my content and the composition of "texts" specific to my content?

Vocabulary: Writing to Learn, Mentor Text

Concept 3: Responding effectively to writing keeps the students writing and moves them forward in their writing skills.

Lesson Essential Question: How do teachers go about responding to writing in a way that encourages students to keep engaging with writing and to hone their writing skills?

Vocabulary: Responding, Assessment, Facilitative Comments, Directive Comments

FIGURE 2.2. RIGOROUS WRITING ASSIGNMENTS

Activity 1: Make a list of all of the "small" writings you've used in your class over the past unit of study. These may include quick writes, writing into the day, passages of reading, explanations of math problems, word problems, student-created definitions of terms, short answers on a pretest, dialectic journals, multi-genre responses to discussions of readings, written responses or reflections on launch activities, and responses in Cornell notes. Be as specific as possible about the intent of these writings. What were the students supposed to be thinking about in connection to your content in each of these writings?

Activity 2: Identify common themes or threads amongst these writings. Try to find more than one. Don't think in terms of writing prompts. Think in terms of bigger things, such as your "essential question" for the unit, or one of the major concepts, or perhaps a concept that will reappear across several units. Also think about the "texts" of your specific content area that you want your students to learn to read AND compose.

Activity 3: OR do this whole thing backward for your next unit. Start with the "essential question" or major concepts and "texts" and think of "small" writings you can use to get kids thinking and reflecting about different layers of that concept.

With the adoption of the computerized writing program Achieve3000, time for Writing Project conceptions of writing became unavailable because all writing time in the school day was dedicated to the program. We were only able to do the first of our planned series of workshops. Our plan had been to have teachers come back in with samples from the assignments they had created from the first workshop and analyze them together to examine the idea of rigor as they had conceived of it in their definitions in workshop 1, and to ensure that standards were being met. We then hoped the teachers would work together, sharing assignments they had written, in order to create more writing assignments that they felt were rigorous and met the standards they needed to teach.

Instead, we saw students spending their writing time regurgitating the ideas presented them by the software company rather than thinking, questioning, and composing about their thoughts on the content they were learning. We didn't see them moving anywhere at all, just simply turning in endless circles.

We continued to work with a few individual teachers, on the margins, as we bumped into them in the halls, but we were puzzled and frustrated. They would ask us for something to do, such as an activity or lesson plan, while we wanted them to think more holistically about changing their practices as writing teachers. The teachers who were "with us" had bought into our idea of successful writing instruction and were using our teaching materials, but they had not changed their thinking in a way that would allow them to craft more ideas and lessons together. In our minds, they were still on the wrong road, one that zig-zagged between our road and the road of the administrators like a path to nowhere. The numbers of those teachers buying into our narrative dwindled as they were administratively reassigned or left the school for other jobs. In the end, the teachers we had worked most closely with left the school during the third year of the study. The multiple-choice test scores still marked the school as low-performing, and we were told that no one in the school had time for writing at all. We wondered what, if anything, we'd actually done there.

ROSA PARKS MIDDLE SCHOOL THROUGH THE ADMINISTRATORS' EYES

The principals of Rosa Parks Middle School were invested in turning around the lives of the children in the neighborhood according to official federal, state, and district mandates. I place emphasis here on turning around because the images counter to those of the pop-culture imagination of an urban school at Rosa Parks Middle School put pressure on the culture of the school to be different, and to move in a different direction from the surrounding environment. The school was built in the center of a high-poverty neighborhood that appeared in the local paper and on the six o'clock news nearly nightly with reports of shootings or other violent crimes. The two principals we worked with wanted Rosa Parks Middle School to be different, and so they set out to build this school as a safe haven for the equitable education of the neighborhood children.

STRUCTURES FOR STUDENTS

Rosa Parks Middle School's district places a heavy emphasis on Safe and Orderly Schools, which is a rating on an annual report card published by the district about each school in the at the end of the year. As a part of creating this safe and orderly environment in the midst of a poor and violent neighborhood, the students at Rosa Parks Middle School wore school uniforms. The district leadership knew that the majority of students would come from families who were struggling to make ends meet. They also knew that in this neighborhood, gang activity was prolific and that middle school–aged children were in danger of being swept up into that lifestyle. Ideally, school uniforms would equalize things for the poorer students and keep them safe from gang activity and disputes over designer clothes, while also enabling students to come to school prepared to do the job of learning—much in the same way adults dress in professional attire for work.

Dr. Carter, the founding principal of the school, was a middle-aged white man and very successful in his leadership of an elementary school serving this same neighborhood. He brought some of those traditions with him to Rosa Parks Middle School. In the elementary school, the staff evoked students' imaginations when they wanted them to move from their classroom to the lunchroom by asking them to pretend to make "duck tails" with their hands and "bubble lips" with their mouths as they moved through the halls. This same idea was part of the culture of Rosa Parks. However, the lines still needed a bit of structure, so the children were asked to walk on the second linoleum block from the wall. Having hands in place, lips together, the orderly lined transitions eliminated pushing or racing to classes. Dr. Carter also gave the teachers megaphones to help make themselves heard over the din of middle schoolers who were not remembering to maintain their duck lips, reminding them to keep their hands in place and move on to their next assignments.

The students moved about the building in this manner to the restroom, the lunchroom, and to supervised recess. The lunchroom was also orderly and quiet. Teachers were assigned lunchroom supervision to monitor behavior and enforce silent lunch for students who had exhibited inappropriate behavior earlier in the day. The children were not allowed to take home the school's textbooks because the risk of losing them was too great; there were few parents home after school to help their children with schoolwork. The lockers were left empty and unassigned because middle-school children might loiter there and/or stash contraband. All of these rules were in place to create order in juxtaposition to the disorder that might be in the students' lives in the neighborhood.

STRUCTURES FOR TEACHERS AND CONSULTANTS

The teachers and the staff felt connected to Dr. Carter. He was devoted to and protective of his staff and students. He understood and accepted the job the district charged him with, which was to turn around the lives of his students by raising scores and creating an orderly, predictable learning environment. He identified himself as a bit of a maverick, unlike many of the administrators at the district level who didn't understand and expect enough of the neighborhood kids. In the first few years Rosa Parks Middle School was open, however, he had been unable to raise the test scores, which he saw as "problematic" and "not indicative of what these kids can do." He often spoke of the faith he had in each of them and the importance of that faith in the "tough" environment—the tough culture—in which they worked, studied, and lived. He saw the school surrounded by conflict, so he wanted to make the school a place of shared purpose, even camaraderie, among the students and the staff.

Dr. Carter was not familiar with the Writing Project, but he agreed to be a part of the grant program because a trusted mentor encouraged him to do so. He knew that the school's writing scores were low, and he hoped that our group would be able to help. He viewed us as just one of the many intervention teams in the school, and he handed us over to his academic facilitator and English department head to facilitate and organize our work. However, he made himself available to talk to us when we asked, and over time we found ourselves connected with him in the same way the staff and students were. He also began to recognize us as being "on his team" and scooped us under his protective shield.

At the end of the second year of the Writing Project–Rosa Parks Middle School partnership, Dr. Carter was asked to use his experience to open a new magnet school in the district and so the district assigned a new principal in the school's fifth year. Despite the efforts of Dr. Carter, the Writing Project, teachers, and other intervention teams from the state, test scores still marked the school as "low performing." The new principal, Principal Morgan, a black woman who had proven herself to be an effective and efficient leader in a district-level position, used the strategic staffing privileges afforded to her with the new job (a privilege Dr. Carter did not have). Strategic staffing made it possible for her to to make quick decisions to remove teachers and administrators and bring in those she felt better suited her leadership style and the needs of the students. She could do this without going through the usual review process that involved mountains of paperwork and consultations with the district office. She committed herself to understanding every aspect of each of the constantly shifting and moving parts of the school and then making that information easily accessible to her teachers and staff. She was also committed to streamlining the many, often conflicting, initiatives at work in the school. In interviews and meetings she often mentioned that her teachers were "pulled in so many directions" and that she wanted them heading in the same "correct" direction together. She viewed Tallulah, Lauren, and I, and the Writing Project at large, as just one more group overburdening already busy teachers with more to do.

Students and staff alike always addressed Principal Morgan formally, and she saw decorum among both as integral to the creation of a safe and orderly learning environment. The megaphones were abolished on her first day in charge, though she kept the orderly transition procedures of hands behind one's back and mouths closed. She brought order to the staff as well. In a staff meeting in the second week of her administration, she reminded teachers of their duty to come to work each day, on time. She also reminded them that sick days, by law, were not to be used for other personal reasons. She insisted on quiet, attentive behavior in all staff meetings and team planning meetings, which were carefully planned, organized, and supervised by the administrative staff. In order to ensure that the time was being used wisely by both the teachers and the consultants, the administrative staff also attended the professional development sessions that Tallulah, Lauren, and I led.

STRUCTURES FOR WRITING

The school's "low performing" designation, due to the fact that the students were not able to show annual yearly progress on their standardized state assessments, made the assessments the focus of instruction in the principals' eyes. Those scores were of the utmost importance for students to move on to high school and for teachers and administrators to keep their jobs and receive bonus pay. For that reason, when Tallulah, Lauren, and I first came to Rosa Parks Middle School, writing and writing instruction happened solely in 7th-grade English/language arts classes, for which students took the state-mandated writing test. The ELA classes in grades 6 and 8 and other content area courses focused on the multiple-choice reading and math state assessments. The 7th-grade students practiced writing the structured essay, which included:

- a thesis statement,
- a main idea at the beginning of each paragraph,
- three pieces of evidence to support the main idea,
- and a conclusion.

Each paragraph was to have three sentences and each paper should have four to five paragraphs.

The state began to require writing in all subject areas shortly after we arrived, and so the teachers worked to bring these structures to other classes to help the students succeed on the test. Further, after the switch in administrators, the new assistant principal in charge of literacy instruction felt that she should raise the bar for writing by insisting that argument be taught in all classes at all grade levels. She was focused on CCSS 8.1 for writing, which places an emphasis on argumentative writing in the 8th grade. She wanted all of the students to reach beyond doing well on the test at their grade level and also be prepared for college-level writing. In a planning meeting, she explained to Tallulah, Lauren, and I that she did not want the students' or teachers' valuable instructional time to be wasted on writing that would not help them attain that important goal.

Additionally, in the second year, a computerized literacy program, Achieve3000, was purchased and adopted in order to help the teachers and students work on writing in a more efficient manner. When the pressures of the state tests approached, Achieve3000 became the most important writing experience for the students because there was no more time available during the school day for writing of any other kind. This was because the administrators made a decision to focus on the multiple-choice standardized tests that would mark their school as either low-performing, growing, or excelling. The program entailed reading a nonfiction piece and filling in blanks with notes from the piece in order to form an essay.

MOVING TOWARD ANALYSIS

These two preceding narratives show the school in two different ways. The administrator's story is the power story constructed by the district and the standards that they answer to.

They have the power to say the school is going to focus on testing and accountability and use prescriptive programs to do so. The consultant's narrative offers a critique of the testing-and-accountability, order-and-control narrative. But that story is suppressed and dismissed as the "do-gooder's" story of the school, especially when Principal Morgan took over. The corporate order-and-control narrative is written on the children's bodies and takes over the teachers' days and curricula, which I talk about in the next chapter. The consultants' narrative makes the teachers' work more difficult because they are thus resisting the administrators' narrative. In the next chapter, I show how the curriculum planning matrix creates order and control over the teachers' lives in the same way the uniforms enact order and control over the students' lives.

Both the administrators' and consultants' narratives offer teachers and students things that will help them turn in the right direction of education. The administrators offer predictability, efficiency, and order. The consultants offer an empty daybook to be filled with critical thinking connected to the students' and teachers' lives, and they offer ways to take that writing further into larger pieces of writing that would fit the teachers' definition of rigor. In both cases, the narratives placed the burden of blame for low test scores on teachers and students for not understanding the different directions in which they were being asked to turn. Rather than helping students, these narratives essentially said that teachers and students were solidifying their social positions—as people who don't take advantage of what is offered them, thus making it their fault that they live in a poor and violent neighborhood with little or no hope of moving out. Neither the administrators nor the consultants took into consideration the impact of such conflicting stories about where to turn and what to do.

The urban school reform narrative illustrates what Foucault (1977) calls the great normalizing institution of school, which works to legitimize the privileged group's perspective on the direction schools need to turn to in order to succeed and the literacy commodities they need to understand in order to find the path. At Rosa Parks Middle School, the normalizing narrative of testing and accountability served to produce and reproduce the hegemonic power and position of the privilege of corporate-produced standardized tests. The teachers, consultants, and even the principals had no institutional power to change the focus on testing or to privilege other values in student learning. Their work would be seen and understood by the central office administration and the state's education department as productive only in terms of students' scores on standardized measures. In that narrative, Rosa Parks Middle School was failing and there was no room for critical and creative thinking—only doing as one is told, following directions, and practicing for standardized tests. In the narrative of urban school reform, these poor, low-performing students needed to acquire certain skills so that they could perform well on standardized tests. They needed to fill in blanks, write to formulas, and get their grammar right. They were not allowed the critical thinking and creativity that I observed in their more affluent counterparts down the street who, because of their class and racial backgrounds, already spoke standard American English and knew the social rituals of the middle class. They already had the skills that Rosa Parks Middle School students "lacked," and they were allowed to be creative and to think critically and work within the narrative that corporate America assigned to them (the narrative of students who perform well on standardized measures). In Rosa Parks Middle School, the corporate narrative worked to produce a certain way of being and knowing. In the following chapter I will examine in more detail how this narrative is inscribed on the actual bodies of the students and produces certain ways of working. I also show how the teachers, students, consultants, and principals worked within and against this narrative via competing narratives of teaching and learning.

3:

MAPPING SOCIAL REPRODUCTION
COMPETING SYSTEMS OF ORDER AND CONTROL

I was signing into the office for a day of professional development at Rosa Parks Middle School when a young African American girl was standing at the counter with her mother. The secretary was explaining the school's uniform policy to her. The girls were supposed to wear khaki slacks or skirts that were no more than four inches above the knee and light blue polo shirts. The girl was looking far less than enthusiastic in the face of this information when the secretary put her hand on her arm and said in a conspiratory whisper, "Girl, you can accessorize!" This brought a shadow of a smile to the young face as the girl plotted her wardrobe.

I was struck by the way the uniform policy created efficiency, order, and control over the way students expressed themselves through dress, while "accessorizing" allowed some flexibility in the policy.

My own children attended an elementary school with a uniform policy much like the one at Rosa Parks Middle School. In my experience as a parent, the uniform certainly made getting children ready for school in the morning simpler, as there were fewer choices to make. It also made shopping for school clothes easy for the same reasons. Those who argue for school uniforms see them as a way of eliminating the distraction of clothing and comparisons between students' socioeconomic status. Uniforms are also seen as a way to prevent gang violence by limiting gang-related apparel (Joseph, 1986; Kaiser, 1985; Stanley, 1996).

However, that morning in the office as the secretary talked with the young girl about accessorizing her uniform (and each morning as my daughter put on the wildest tights we could find), I was seeing the human relationship that was evident in the accessorizing policy. That narrative claimed that the student was good and valuable just the way she was, that the choices she made about her dress and the narratives about culture that those choices represent are valued in this school. The accessorizing policy was unofficial while the uniform policy was official. The staff simply turned a blind eye to uniform infractions.

There is scholarship arguing that uniforms simply paper over the problems of poverty and violence that the students face in their daily lives (DeMitchell, 2006; Kohn, 1998; Yeung, 2009). In my children's school as well as at Rosa Parks, I saw evidence of these arguments in the way that some students had polo shirts from Lands' End and Gap while others had shirts from Walmart and Target. Some students' uniforms were fresh and new, while others were worn and old. Some students wore certain colors in their accessories to identify themselves with social groups.

In its quest to eliminate trouble, Rosa Parks Middle School inscribed the narrative of efficiency, order, and control directly onto the bodies of the students by determining and prescribing precisely what the children should wear. The way the staff allowed the students to accessorize, seemingly with no limits as long as they were wearing the required shirts and pants or skirts, was emblematic of the way the students and teachers negotiated the testing and accountability narrative as it is caught up in the urban school reform narrative (the power narrative) with other narratives of ways to be in the world, such as the young girl's desire to pick out her own clothing.

As I thought about the uniform policy, I thought about the other ways we had noticed the school exhibiting order and control over student behavior. I thought of the students changing classes in straight lines walking two blocks over from the walls in order to avoid scuffing them, with their hands behind their backs and their lips closed. I thought about how different this was from other middle schools in the district where students bubbled out into the hallway during class change laughing and talking with friends.

As I was reflecting on these images of order and control over students, I noticed a planning matrix on the wall. It was a carefully constructed document accounting for each teacher's planning period and the time after students left for the day. Each block detailed how that time would be spent and parsed out the work of the school over the course of the week. The planning matrix brought uniformity to teachers' time outside of class, ensuring that they were all doing the same types of planning together at the same time.

And yet as a teacher myself, I was horrified to see that there was very little empty planning space in which a teacher could grade papers, plan lessons, and reflect on the day's work alone and with colleagues. I wondered how the teachers found the time to do this essential work of teaching. I thought of the teachers I saw at Rosa Parks Middle School huddled in the hallway whispering together and the long hours of work after school and at home that they told me about. To me, these observations and my own ideas about teacher time represented a different narrative from the one promoted by the planning matrix, and the two narratives were in conflict.

In this school, the power narrative and forms of resistance to it that we saw in the uniform policy were also exhibited in the school's curriculum planning. The dominant testing and accountability narrative is caught up in efficiency, order, and control because those values are seen as common-sense ways to obtain high test scores and prove accountability. However, as I will illustrate in this chapter, what is created is often simply a façade of order and control, and teachers' and students' resistance illuminates the social reproduction that traps students in the status quo.

Standing there that morning, it occurred to me that I was in a school that valued uniformity in dress and teaching. The testing and accountability narrative sees uniformity as a good thing. Its purpose is to make sure that every student is receiving an equal education. According to the testing and accountability narrative, if all students are given a level playing field through measures like uniformity in dress and uniformity in teaching, they will succeed. The order and control emphasized by such policies feeds into the promise that if you do what you are told you will get ahead, so why didn't it seem to be working in this school, where test scores named it low performing? This question, along with the narrative of efficiency, order, and control, seemed to surround me that morning as I carefully signed into the office and waited for a security guard to escort me to the classroom I meant to visit.

In this chapter I use activity theory to examine the school uniforms and the planning matrix in order to map how these narrative negotiations happen. In each of these illuminating moments, other figured worlds and their narratives, such as the students' and teachers' ideas about how adolescents should dress and the teachers' ideas about the best way to plan and teach, intersect with that of the school, creating tension. In these moments, the reproductive power of the dominant group—as represented by the urban school reform narrative's focus on testing and accountability—is visible in that the ideas of order and control create very narrow understandings of what counts as knowledge in schools.

ACTIVITY THEORY AND FIGURED WORLDS: TOOLS FOR ANALYSIS

Activity theory originates in the cultural-historical school of Russian psychology with the work of Vygotsky and Leontiev and Luria. Leontiev named the theory, which relies heavily on Vygotsky's developmental concept of *zones of proximal development*. This concept makes a distinction between what a child can do on her own and what a child can do with mediating tools and the help of those around her. It affords a method with which to examine the multilayered, multivoiced ways that people use to construct their worlds and the material reality that is created as a result. It affords a way to look at the multiple narratives acting on people all at the same time. It affords a way to look at the multiple narratives acting on students as they get dressed in the mornings and teachers as they work, to isolate the different narratives they are negotiating and think about the material results of that negotiation. It affords a way to look at the world through a critical postmodern lens (Engestrom, Miettinen & Punamaki, 1999).

The complicated and conflicting narratives about school uniforms and teacher planning time that the students and teachers are negotiating in the paragraphs above are part of an *activity system*. Activity systems are "goal directed, historically situated, cooperative human interactions" (Russell, 1995, p. 53). In the case of uniforms, the student is involved in the activity system of getting dressed for school, but that activity system is intersecting with the other activity systems of the school and outside of the school such as the activity systems of her neighborhood and family in which the girl is involved. Also, the young student in the narrative above is more than just a girl. She is a *subject*. In the critical postmodern lens the subject is more than just a person. She is constructed of many different *discourses*. These discourses are not merely represented through spoken language or text "but involve habituated and largely unconscious ways of thinking, talking, feeling, acting, and being" (Kamberelis & Dimitriadis, 2005, p. 48) that circulate in the different activity systems she inhabits.

Different discourses have differing amounts of power. The discourses acting on the student as she decides what to wear to school have differing amounts of power. These discourses "both literally and metaphorically inscribe/produce the individual and the collective social body" (Kamberelis & Dimitriadis, 2005, p. 48). The critical postmodern lens sees the subject (the student) as constructed by Foucault's discursive systems (language being representative of meaning and a producer of knowledge and power rather than the "Truth") and articulating multiple subjectivities (because discourse is merely representative, people are acting as different representations of the subject all at the same time). It affords an analysis of the dialogic construction happening between the *sites of multiple subjectivities* people enact. Sites of multiple subjectivity refer to the ways in which subjects are "always being produced at the intersection of multiple discursive and material forces" (Kamberelis & Dimitriadis, 2005, p. 49). Activity theory allows us to examine all of these different sites of subjectivity and the way they intersect, as the student gets dressed for school and teachers do the work of planning. We can see the discursive and material forces of the various narratives at work, acting on the teachers and student when the student dresses for school and the teachers plan. We can see the way in which the discourses of power are producing the student and the teachers as well as the way in which other conflicting discourses of culture, family, and conflicting ideas about what it means to plan as a teacher are producing them, as all of these narratives are in dialogue with one another.

All that said, the student has choices about how to interpret the way the discourses of power are positioning her through the school uniform and reimagine her context through her accessories (Kamberelis & Dimitriadis, 2005). The teachers also have choices about how to interpret the way they are being positioned by the planning matrix. Activity theory views human agency as a factor in the construction of the world. As a methodology, it answers the critique that postmodern thought does not attend to the actual material reality of people interacting socially, historically, and culturally. Critics say that the representation of truth rather than the concept of Truth does not give people any control over their lives in any real way. Activity theory offers a way to analyze that control.

In my use of activity theory, I draw heavily on Holland et al.'s (1998) concept of figured worlds, as described in Chapter 2. Holland et al. describe how people can have a "modicum of agency or control over their own behavior" when they understand themselves as actors in "socially and culturally constructed worlds" and make use of Vygotsky's mediating tools to change that behavior (p. 40). Holland et al. call these "socially produced, culturally constructed activities," figured worlds leaning heavily on Leontiev's understanding of activity when they do so (p. 41). To avoid cluttering the text, and to bring together activity theory with the theory of figured worlds that I introduced in Chapter 2, I will use the term *figured world* to describe activity systems. Holland et al. add a careful extension to the examination of the division of labor in activity systems with their understanding of figured worlds. They explain that the identifiable social types and roles through which people are distributed in the division of labor are not abstract, but are "specifically historical developments, grown through continued participation in the positions defined by the social organization of those world's activity" (p. 41). This sociohistorical positioning acknowledges the modicum of agency in figured worlds, as people are actors as well as subjects depending upon their use of mediating tools. The idea of mediating tools is key to understanding the narratives of the socializing activity of schooling in the United States, as the tools are intersecting and in dialogue with the figured world of Rosa Parks Middle School. These dialogues, intersections, and conflicts, and the ways in which they are using the same mediating tools but with different goals and differing outcomes, represent the productive tensions within the narratives in the figured world of Rosa Parks Middle School. These tensions hold the potential for transformation, rather than social reproduction.

In this study, activity theory serves as a way to set the case study of Rosa Parks Middle School, and particularly four students and two teachers, against the background of urban school reform. It serves as a way to examine the complexity of the multiple intersecting and conflicting narratives that students, teachers, consultants, and administrators are negotiating as they figure out how to be in the figured world of the school. Below I will examine the mediating tools of school uniforms and the planning matrix and the intersecting figured worlds of the teachers, students, consultants, and administrators within Rosa Parks Middle School.

SCHOOL UNIFORMS: INSCRIBING NARRATIVE THEORIES-IN-USE ON STUDENTS' BODIES

Engestrom's (in Engestrom, Miettinen & Punamaki, 1999) model of activity theory in Figure 3.1 acts as a metaphor for the social relations that make up activity systems. The double-ended arrows illustrate the ways in which Subjects, Tools, Rules, Community, Division of Labor, and Objects are all in constant dialogue to make up the Outcomes, which are ways of being in the activity system. These ways of being are continually being created and make up the material reality of what people are doing (how people are behaving) in any one moment. The triangle represents one activity system, but there are multiple activity systems overlapping and interlocking all the time. Table 3.1 defines each of the elements of activity theory and gives an example in the case of the mediating tool of school uniforms. These examples are not inclusive of all of the activity in the activity system of Rosa Parks Middle School in regards to school uniforms, but merely one or two aspects of that. A fuller picture of how uniforms are working in the figured world of Rosa Parks Middle School will follow.

FIGURE 3.1. MODEL OF ACTIVITY THEORY

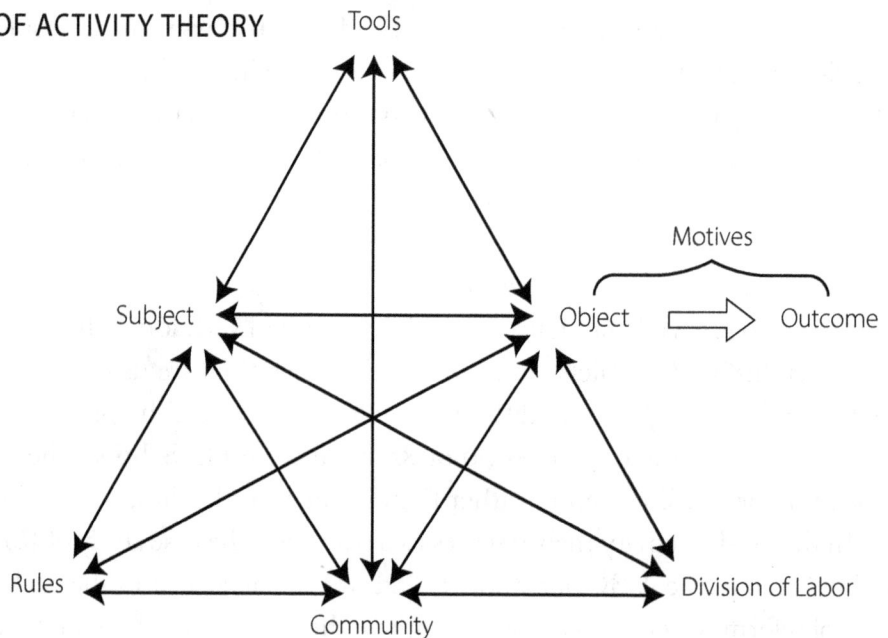

TABLE 3.1. ACTIVITY THEORY DEFINITIONS AND EXAMPLES

Activity	Definition	Examples
Tools	Physical objects and systems of symbols (like language, mathematics) that people use to accomplish the activity	School Uniforms
Subject	Person or people engaged in activity who are the focus of a study on activity. The point of view used to focus on the activity. (See the definition of subject in the text above for the complexity of the term as opposed to person.)	Students, Administrators, Teachers
Motives	Purposes, reasons for the activity	Student motives: identity construction Administration motives: keeping students safe
Object	Problem space	Students: struggle for identity Administrators: danger for students
Outcome	Desired goals of activity	Students: identity construction Administrators: student safety
Rules	Laws, codes, conventions, customs, and agreements that people adhere to while engaging in the activity	Ideas of uniform dress for students as a safety measure and an equalizer in terms of income
Community	People and groups whose knowledge, interests, stakes, and goals shape the activity	The people in the neighborhood, stakeholders in the school
Division of Labor	How the work in the activity is divided among participants in the activity	The people who decide what the uniforms will look like and who will wear them

The uniforms of Rosa Parks Middle School are illustrative of how narratives for participating in the role of student are literally inscribed upon the bodies of the students through the order and control of student dress. To illustrate the competing narratives at work in the construction of the student role at Rosa Parks Middle School and how the uniforms reproduce the dominant power narrative and paper over issues of poverty and violence in the students' lives, I take a look at how the uniform policy was created, how the uniforms were chosen and designed, and how the uniform code is actually interpreted and enforced by the students and the staff of the school.

The Rosa Parks Middle School uniforms are light-blue collared polo shirts and khaki pants or skirts, modeled after retail management attire. The uniform policy states that students' shirts must have collars, and that pants, skirts, and shorts must be no more than six inches above the knee and must be belted at the natural waistline.

Creativity and noncompliance through dress are considered deviant behaviors by the school district, who says that these kids need uniforms. Standardization, order, and compliance are the desired outcome of the mediating tool of school uniforms. Rosa Parks Middle School has a uniform policy because of its low-performing, at-risk status. The fact that other middle schools in the system that serve predominantly upper-middle-class populations are not viewed as needing uniforms marks the Rosa Parks students as deficient in their ability to dress themselves. According to the narrative prescribed by urban school reform in the United States and echoed in conversations with school administrators and in the district officials' positions, uniforms are necessary to standardize dress and to prevent distractions from learning—distractions such as socioeconomic differences, sexually or inappropriately revealing clothing, or gang colors. These conversations are represented in the literature I mentioned in the introduction to this chapter as well as in the conversations I had with the school administrators and district-level leaders visiting the school about why these students were wearing uniforms. These same distractions are of course present in all schools, but they are considered a problem that must be addressed in *this* school because it is considered low performing.

The uniform style was chosen by the school system in accordance with the school colors and the social rules found in the urban school reform narrative about school uniforms in U.S. public schools, which differ from the private prep school uniforms with blazers, ties, and knee socks. These differences in requirements symbolize the difference between the retail management or service worker and the suit- and tie-wearing CEO.

Another figured world that intersects with that of the school is the large high-end, family-owned regional department store helping the underprivileged children. The company donated the designs for the polo shirts as a complement to the plain version available at discount department stores. Students voted on designs that were approved by the school board, and then the store donated one shirt in that design to each student.

The winning design has the school emblem embroidered on it along with an argyle stripe. Students' families can purchase more of these shirts from the department store through the school. The store has also designed argyle sweater vests to complement the shirts. In this way the students are branded with both the school logo and the department store's argyle.

No other logo is allowed. The store gets nearly free marketing for helping underprivileged children, while corporate values continue to be inscribed on the students' bodies through branded marketing. Corporate values are of course inscribed on students' bodies when they choose to wear name-brand accessories (Nike for example), but here that is the choice of the student rather than a dictate of the school.

The division of labor using the school uniform positions the school district's central office and the dominant knowledge claims of urban reform and public schooling in the United States with the power to decide what the children should wear to school. The central office and school board must approve all uniform designs and colors before the school administrators can make their choices. In the case of the department store designs the children voted on, the only choices where those sanctioned by the school board. The students, and for that matter the school staff, had no input in the initial designs that were presented for approval. The school administrators and teachers enforce the dress code and the students and their families comply and cooperate.

However, to get a full picture of the way the mediating tool of school uniforms is working to inscribe narratives on the bodies of students, it is necessary to look at the way the narratives of the students, their families, and the school staff construct the figured world of the school through the school uniform. The school staff affords students the ability to accessorize, which takes on the narratives of the students' cultural and historical backgrounds. Some students comply completely with the school's expectation. These students are more often found in the honors classes. Others accessorize with sweatshirts that identify them with their Latino/Latina peers, with hip-hop culture, or with other cultural groups. Some of the girls wear their polo shirts and khaki skirts and pants in form-fitting styles that expose cleavage or accentuate their hips, while some of the boys wear their khaki pants low around their hips, exposing designer-label boxer shorts underneath. Students further accessorize with shoes, jewelry, and hairstyles that identify them as members of different social groups and serve as socioeconomic markers. The result is anything but uniform.

The students' resistance, expressed through their accessorizing of officially sanctioned uniforms, and the staff's unofficial sanctioning of this resistance when they encourage this accessorizing, exhibits tension within the figured world of schooling in the United States. The students and staff are negotiating their culturally and historically formed understandings of ways of being a student in the world of Rosa Parks Middle School with that of the dominant ways of being a student. They are pushing at the boundaries of the power narrative and the statements it makes about the social position the students should be accepting. The students and staff are still recognizable in this power narrative, but with very different ways of using the mediating tools of school uniforms with different motivations (like identity formation) for differing outcomes (non-uniform appearance). The ability to be recognizable can be a productive tension that holds transformative potential for what it means to be a student in the school world, in that it disrupts the reproductive socialization process of the institution of schooling that says these students should accept the deficit social position of not knowing how to dress properly. However, one possible view is that the uniforms don't help because inscribing order and control on students' bodies through dress in this way only reminds the children that they are not good enough. They must be helped to know how to be and what to wear.

PLANNING MEETINGS: ORDER AND CONTROL OVER TEACHERS

The instructional planning meetings at Rosa Parks Middle School, particularly after the district appointed Mrs. Morgan as principal, illustrate how competing narratives of order and control construct the role of teacher in the figured world of the school. These narratives offer competing views of knowledge in the school: what counts and who decides.

Since the school's founding, teachers at Rosa Parks Middle School were expected to plan curriculum together during scheduled meetings. Administrators also reviewed and planned with teachers regularly. However, when Mrs. Morgan started, tasked with the job of turning the school around, she chose to use the activity of teacher planning to create careful surveillance of the teachers' work, thereby exerting more order and control over them.

At the beginning of her first full year of leadership, she and her fellow administrators created a careful matrix of meetings (see Table 3.2) with very specific purposes. The meetings took place during teacher planning periods and after school on Tuesdays and Wednesdays.

An administrator attended and took careful notes at each meeting to ensure that the participants stuck to the required agendas. Teachers were expected to plan and teach with their colleagues so that each student in each course on each grade level experienced the same lessons, at the same time, delivered in the same way. This kind of planning was to be discussed in the meetings rather than less formally in the halls, when teachers were supposed to be monitoring students. In this way, the administration hoped to ensure that every student in every class received equal instruction. The administrators' participation was meant to ensure the quality of that instruction by being a part of the lesson planning.

Teachers turned in their lesson plans in a form specified by the school. On the form teachers were asked to list each standard they were planning to teach in a unit, complete with a description of the standard. Then they were asked to break down each day with

TABLE 3.2. PLANNING MATRIX

	Monday	Tuesday	Wednesday	Thursday	Friday
Block 1	Grade Level Planning 8th grade 8:32–10:00	Content Meeting 8th grade 8:32–10:00 Various Classrooms	Content Meeting 8th grade 8:32–10:00 Various Classrooms	CSZ Planning or Individual Planning [CSZ: Central Secondary Zone (Math/LA only)]	Team Meeting/ Parent Conferences Various Classrooms
Block 2	Grade Level Planning 7th grade 10:02–11:30	Content Meeting 7th grade 10:02–11:30 Various Classrooms	Content Meeting 7th grade 10:02–11:30 Various Classrooms	CSZ Planning or Individual Planning	Team Meeting/ Parent Conferences Various Classrooms
Block 3	Elective Team Planning 11:32–1:30	Elective Content Planning 11:32–1:30 Various Classrooms	Elective Content Planning 11:32–1:30 Various Classrooms	CSZ Planning or Individual Planning	Team Meeting/ Parent Conferences Various Classrooms
Block 4	Grade Level Planning 6th grade 1:32–3:00	Content Meeting 6th grade 1:32–3:00 Various Classrooms	Content Meeting 6th grade 1:32–3:00 Various Classrooms	CSZ Planning or Individual Planning	Team Meeting/ Parent Conferences Various Classrooms

Monthly Meetings	Tuesday		Wednesday
PM Meetings, 3:30	**"MANTRA" Meeting (PD)**	**Admin. Meeting**	New Teacher Meeting 1st Tuesday of each month Mentor/Mentee Monthly Meeting 3:30 in Media Center
	1st, 2nd, and 5th Wednesday of each month (Mandatory Attendance)		
	Strategic Plan Meeting 3rd Wednesday of each month(Mandatory Attendance)	TIER Meeting 4th Wednesday of each month (Mandatory Attendance)	

Monthly Content Meetings	Subject
2nd Tuesday of each month, 3:30	LA, Math, Science, Social Studies
3rd Wednesday of each month, 3:30	Performance Management, Increasing the Graduation Rate, Teaching and Learning Through Technology, Environmental Stewardship, Parent and Community Connections

Content Meetings: All grade levels teaching a specific content meet
Grade Level Planning: All teachers in a specific grade, no matter the subject, meet
Central Secondary Zone Meetings: All math and Language Arts teachers meet with the central office math and Language Arts leaders
Team Meeting/Parent Conferences: Teachers teaching the same students meet and conference with parents
"MANTRA" Meeting: Full staff meets together with administrative team.
Strategic Plan Meeting: Committees meet to work toward the school's strategic plan to raise test scores

the standards that would be taught that day and a complete description of what would be happening in the class and how those activities related to the standards. Finally, for each day they were to explain "students will be able to," detailing the outcome of each lesson and how the students would show that they had met the standards. The administrators sat in on the planning meetings to discuss and critique the plans. For the administrators, the planning matrix and planning forms were mediating tools to ensure the outcome of order and control over the teachers' activity, as well as to ensure uniformity in information delivery and defining what counts as knowledge in each classroom.

The teachers were only officially allowed to talk to one another in these supervised planning meetings; casual conversation was forbidden, and the talking was expected to follow a protocol put in place to ensure uniformity. Any disruption to the agenda, whether that was talking about an objective out of order, sharing a personal story, or talking about students not listed on the agenda, was not allowed. Teachers were immediately verbally reprimanded for breaking these rules.

The planning matrix and the careful supervision of meetings and lesson planning places the value on uniformity in instruction, offering one specific view of what should be happening in the classroom. Creativity in planning and non-compliance with agendas was considered deviant behavior. The activity of planning and teaching in the building creates an environment where teachers are not trusted to think as professionals and know what their students might need at any given moment. They are to follow the careful agenda to plan a lesson that they all must teach. The assumption is that all students and teachers are the same and that knowledge is a commodified thing that students and teachers get. Another logical conclusion from this setup is that if teachers are not carefully told what to do and then carefully watched, they will not do their jobs; they will not teach.

Within the division of power, we as writing consultants also had a role in the planning activities at Rosa Parks Middle School. We brought a competing value system that applied to teachers' roles in the activity of planning, which held the core idea of teachers teaching teachers, based on the Writing Project values and our understanding of Paulo Freire's (1997) problem-posing, dialogic education. We felt that endless meetings during teachers' planning periods were wasting the teachers' time. We wanted to refigure that time by using it for professional development. However, while we were operating in the narrative that our information was important enough to share during this time, the administrators were not. Though we asked the teachers what they would like to work with in regards to writing instruction, we did not provide much space for their ideas when we didn't like their answers (e.g., when they focused on testing and assessment). We were attempting to control planning and curriculum by coming to planning meetings with our own set agendas for the time, expecting the teachers and administrators to follow it. We expected the teachers to excitedly embrace our notions of writing and writing instruction, where writing was about thinking critically and writing instruction was about teaching students to get their ideas out of their heads and down on paper. Our narrative was that the students and teachers would want to be pushed to critique the power structures at work in their lives. We had to constantly remind ourselves to consider the differing stakes of such critique for white middle-class women with university jobs and minority administrators, teachers, and students working and learning in a school constructed as failing in the midst of a neighborhood constructed as violent and dangerous.

Tallulah and I struggled to listen to the teachers and administrators when they pointed this out to us, saying that we were "do-gooders" who did not expect enough from the students. We slipped time and time again into a deficit construction of the dissenting administrators and teachers when we became frustrated with teachers and administrators not accepting what we wanted to offer. We continually had to work with our colleagues at the Writing Project outside of the school to re-affix our own critical lenses to see the material reality of the tensions that the teachers and administrators pointed out to us. While our brand of surveillance over the teachers did not involve bullhorns or pink slips, it was there in our affirmations of "good job" to those who did what we suggested, and our pursed lips and red faces, or "no, but" conversations masked in "what if" phraseology when others resisted.

The figured world of the testing industry in the United States also intersects with the planning meeting at Rosa Parks Middle School. Students' performance on state-level tests marked the school as "failing" and in need of intervention, which took the form of administrators' careful monitoring of planning and instruction. The tests were created at the state level by "recruited educators trained to create tests" and "professional item writers" (Public Schools of North Carolina, Accountability Division). The people training the teachers and the professional item writers represent the testing industry. The agendas of the planning meetings were based on covering testing standards and collecting data in the form of practice tests to show whether the children had mastered the standards. In this way, it is the outsider test-makers who determine what will be discussed in the meetings, what will be taught in classes, and what counts as knowledge.

The division of labor in the use of the mediating tool of "planning meetings" within the figured world of Rosa Parks Middle School imbues the testing industry with the power to decide what teachers should be teaching and what children should be learning. The administrators then have the power to decide how information will be delivered. Outsiders like ourselves as consultants were allowed to have a voice in the interventions, but anything we offered that did not directly address testing in the eyes of the administrators was dismissed. The teachers had very limited power over what they taught, especially if it differed from the ideas of the testing industry and the administrators. Students and their families had no power in determining what is taught. The administrators must carefully watch the teachers' planning and teaching. Teams from the state and the district must carefully watch the administrators. The success of all of this watching is measured by the test creators. And in our case as consultants, the success of our "watching" was measured by the research corporation that evaluates the Writing Project.

At once in compliance with and resistant to the controlled planning, the teachers developed a policy of off-the-clock sharing. The narrative represented by this policy is that the official meetings are a performance of the administrative-sanctioned planning. The real planning has to happen around the margins of the workday. The teachers who came to see us as colleagues talked with us in the halls or after meetings. In my interviews and observations of both official planning meetings and other interactions among teachers, I learned that the teachers texted each other before and after school, as well as during the school day, sometimes surreptitiously under desks during official planning meetings. They whispered together about ideas and students at the start of official planning meetings with one eye on the door, ready to defend their behavior should an administrator come in. They also critiqued the uniformity being demanded of them. Teams of people from the school district and from the state had led several workshops about differentiation, pointing out that each student is different and learns differently and that master teachers are not only aware of these differences, but they structure lessons in such a way as to meet the different needs of each student. The teachers used the language of these teams to explain themselves when they deviated from the scripted lesson or the ways of writing suggested by the consultants. They discovered ways to meet the needs of their students and explain how it fit in with what they had been asked to do. When no one was watching, the teachers reflected, planned, and thought together about what they wanted their students to learn and how they could help them to do that by negotiating and complying with the school's planning and instructional delivery design.

The teachers resisted the order and control imposed on their work environment by the testing industry, administrators, and Writing Project consultants by closing their doors and teaching in ways that they felt, as professionals committed to their students, were important. They participated in the narrative of commodified education by inviting us in when they felt their methods would be sanctioned because they were using a tool or an activity we had given them, and they hoped to use us as leverage for those activities when they went against the administrators' directives. However, they also often felt that our ways were not sanctioned by the school or district administration, and so they discussed them together behind closed doors or on their off time. This is a recognizable and common narrative of resistance for teachers in U.S. schools.

At the same time, the narratives of compliance are also recognizable in the world of schooling in the United States, where teachers are told that if they work hard and do as they are told, their students will pass the test. The narrative also says that if the students don't pass the test, then it is the students who are to blame, not the compliant teacher or the supervising administrator, and certainly not the testing industry itself. The tension exhibited between the various socially and historically constructed narratives of order and control of planning and instruction at work in the different actors in the figured world of Rosa Parks Middle School informs participants' understanding of how to perform the role of teacher (as well as that of administrator, and consultant) in the socializing world of Rosa Parks Middle School and is situated in the reproductive, socializing world of schooling in the United States.

An important tension exists within the urban school reform narrative as the staff at Rosa Parks Middle School, composed predominantly of minority teachers serving a population of poor minority students, are supervised and controlled, while the white teachers in the school down the road serving predominantly white upper-middle-class students talk to one other freely. Teachers in other buildings are constructed as creative and brilliant when they deviate from scripted plans to meet the needs of students, while the deviating teachers at Rosa Parks Middle School were viewed as problems and removed from the school. As white, middle-class actors ourselves, in some ways we wanted the teachers at Rosa Parks Middle School to openly resist the narrative imposed on their planning by the administrators, except when that resistance kept us from controlling the instruction and curriculum in the ways that we felt enabled writing to happen in the school. The teachers carefully negotiated within and against these narratives of control over their planning and instruction in order to teach in ways that they felt were important to students. Their work pushed at the boundaries of the power narrative that says teachers must be controlled and watched in order to ensure they are teaching. The teachers' resistance illuminates the social reproduction of the testing industry that does not see past numbers to individual students and what their needs and talents might be.

NEGOTIATING NARRATIVES TO "BE" TEACHER OR STUDENT

The tensions represented through activity theory in this chapter show how order and control in the school is in many ways simply an illusion. The administrators, consultants, teachers, and students are all pushing at the boundaries imposed on them of what is recognizable as knowledge and knowledge-making. The narrative of order and control papers over reality with the appearance of a happily-ever-after promise of things that will put people on the right path to get out of the poverty forest. Under the paper, consultants are being paid to help with writing in a school where no one writes, the school is in disorder, and the children who all look alike are vastly different.

All of that is quite a bit for a middle school student to negotiate when they are asked to sit down and write in school. This study is focused on various narratives and the negotiation of those narratives in student writing, particularly the narratives that disrupt the socially reproductive narrative of schooling. In Part I, I have developed various narratives in the world of Rosa Parks Middle School. Part II focuses the narrative lens in closer to the figured worlds of two teachers and four of their students at Rosa Parks Middle School in order to examine more closely what it means to be teachers and students in the specific figured world of the school and think about moments of resistance as critiques on the larger system that is trapping them all in poverty through social reproduction.

PART II:

HOW TO "BE" WRITING TEACHERS AND STUDENTS

4:

NARROWING THE LENS

TEACHING AS NARRATIVE NEGOTIATION

One brisk morning in March, I was sitting in my quiet home office surrounded by open books, working on a paper for class (I was in graduate school at the time) when an email popped up in the corner of my screen:

> OMG
> Can you get over here today! [Samuel's] all girls' class has done some *unbelievable writing*. I need to get this published ASAP! We need your help!!!

It was our second year working with Rosa Parks Middle School, and Tallulah and I had facilitated a workshop entitled "Using Genre to Act on Content Area" the day before.

I grabbed the phone, called the school, and managed to get a very excited academic facilitator on the line. She wanted to know if Tallulah or I could come right then. Tallulah and I exchanged some jubilant text messages, and because she happened to be in the area, Tallulah went by. She got there just in time to join the class where the students—mainly African-American girls—were reading aloud from their homework papers: diary entries written as if they were Jewish children living during the Holocaust. The teacher, the academic facilitator, and the new principal, Mrs. Morgan, were all in the room, listening to the girls read with tears in their eyes. When Tallulah entered, the girls greeted her and asked one student, Erin, to read her entry again. As she read quietly, the students and adults openly cried. Several other tearful entries were shared before the period ended.

Afterwards, Tallulah wrote to Lauren and me, thinking about and celebrating this moment that we had been invited into.

When I was getting ready to leave, one of the girls asked [Samuel] something. And he said, I don't know, ask her. She said, "Did you cry listening to the stories?" I said something like "Well you know these diary entries are very powerful and full of emotion. The thing though that is really affecting me is the way that all of you girls are so interested and connected to your writing and that you are doing all of this amazing writing and thinking in social studies with [Samuel]." (And being me) I actually was a little choked up telling them that. I looked over at Samuel and he was tearing up himself. What a moment—teacher, kids, WP consultant connecting over a writing assignment.

This chapter focuses on the narratives of two social studies teachers who are negotiating the various narratives presented in Chapter 3 in order to engage their students in the curriculum of the class through writing. These analyses will then serve as context for the student work in Chapters 5 and 6.

A WORD ABOUT GENRE THEORY: WHAT WE WERE ATTEMPTING TO DO

I want to pause here with a word about genre theory and problematize the workshop we led in order to better explain the assignment Samuel gave. Though Tallulah and I had been studying genre theory and thinking about genres as sites of action rather than simply containers for knowledge, our workshop really dealt with genre as "form." Genre as form is problematic because it lends itself to formulaic writing, where there is a form to be filled out, much like a fill-in-the-blank worksheet. Genre as form smacks of the testing and accountability narrative that we were trying to critique. Genre as sites of action see genre as a place where writers act on something, exploring the rules for behavior in that genre and then acting within those rules while also pushing the boundaries.

Now when I do workshops on genre, I use the analogy of going to a party. One has to figure out the purpose of the party and who will attend in order to know what to wear, what types of conversations are appropriate, and how to behave. Then the person decides how to be recognizable as belonging in this setting while maintaining personal identity and possibly pushing at the boundaries. Entering a genre is much the same, and working with genre in this way requires much more critical thinking than filling in a form.

The title of the workshop alluded to our beginning thinking about genre as sites of action, and on the agenda we had written:

If we think about genres as sites of action, as ways of being and viewing the world, then viewing a topic through different genres and contexts is like holding it up to the light and looking at it from different angles, from different viewpoints.

However, the activity that we asked the teachers to try with each other and later with their students does not really push the term genre past the container notion of form. In fact, we even say "forms/genres" on the handout—marking the terms as interchangeable.

We asked the teachers to work with the handout in Figure 4.1 below.

FIGURE 4.1. WRITING TO LEARN: USING GENRE TO ACT ON COURSE CONTENT

1. Take a moment to think about the topic you are working with in the unit you are teaching right now. Quickly list everything you know about it, or everything you wanted your students to know. (5 min.)

2. Choose one or more of the following forms/genres to show us what you were just writing about. (15 min.)

A free verse poem	A political cartoon
A poem in a character's voice	A Myspace page
A monologue	A series of Facebook status updates
A newspaper article	A video game
A wanted ad	A storyboard for a short film
A resume	A text message conversation
A collection of recipes	A song or collection of songs
A poem in two voices	If this topic were a car, what kind of car would it
A dialogue between two characters	be? What would be the accessories?
A CD song list	If this topic were an outfit, what would it look like?
A comic strip	A genre of your choice

Basically, this activity asks writers to plop what they know about a topic into multiple forms. They aren't acting on anything. And this container idea of genre became obvious in the diary writing assignment that Samuel took away from the activity and that prompted the email message above. He asked the students to write a diary as if they were children of the Holocaust. The students didn't examine the actions available in the act of diary writing or being a child during the Holocaust as I would have had them do when teaching this lesson now, but simply were asked to fill in the form of diary, as they understood it. Looking back with my fuller understanding of genre as a site of action now, I see the formulaic nature of the assignment, but that's hindsight. In the moment, I was jumping out of my skin over having struck a chord with one of the teachers.

NARRATIVES OF CONVERGENCE AND RESISTANCE

Samuel's narrative, the story of the Holocaust diary entries that opened this chapter, is one of convergence, where teachers, consultants, and administrators all work out of the testing and accountability narrative of urban school reform, where teaching and learning is about doing what you are "supposed to do." Samuel was teaching writing because he was supposed to add it into his social studies curriculum, and the administration was excited because both the teacher and the students had done what they were asked. As Writing Project consultants sent to help teachers get more writing into their classrooms, we were also excited because a teacher had done what he was supposed to do and taken something from our workshop to the classroom.

This narrative is about following the rules of the district and producing results; the results here are that all of the students were engaged enough to do their homework. The teachers, administrators, and consultants all offered ways for students to write in social studies class, so according to the testing and accountability narrative, if the students don't produce quality writing, they only have themselves to blame. A tension around the edges of all this conformity lies in the form of the writing we were promoting. While we did fall into the form trap, which can be equated to the formulaic writing of the testing and accountability narrative, the forms we offered were outside of that narrative and could be (and later were) considered play writing by the testing and accountability agenda of the administrators, who made an argument-only writing policy. In fact, this chapter and the chapters following are focused on social studies classes because the English/language arts teachers, who were directly responsible for a reading comprehension test, did not feel that they had time for this play writing while trying to comply with the argument-only writing policy and Achieve3000.

The second narrative in the chapter, focused on Ronald, is one of dual resistance and compliance that further illuminates the tension of a teacher doing what he is "supposed to do" for the consultants. Ronald implemented the daybook (described in detail in Chapter 2) into his 7th-grade social studies class. However, our daybook assignments were outside of the testing and accountability narrative and so he was resisting the dominant narrative of the school as well as the school's argument-only policy.

In both cases as I look at the dual narratives of compliance and resistance and how they work within and against the accountability and testing agenda, I also explore how identity and class are at play as the teachers negotiate their positionality in the school world. Foucault (1977) argues that the institution of school is one of the great normalizing institutions in society. Giroux (1983), Ryan (1991), and Ayers and Ayers (2011) are just a few of the scholars who build on Foucault's ideas to illustrate the great socializing process of schooling. As I've described in Chapter 3, there are multiple and, in many cases, conflicting narratives of schooling within the figured world of Rosa Parks Middle School, with the dominant one being the testing and accountability narrative of urban school reform. In order for teachers and students to be recognized in the school world, they must negotiate these conflicting narratives that are inscribed on them along with the lived narratives of their histories in order to compose themselves, or their identities, as teachers and students.

THEORIES FOR CONSTRUCTING IDENTITIES

Identity construction has everything to do with the way educators think about teaching, learning, and writing instruction as the work within and against the testing and accountability narrative of urban school reform. The teachers at Rosa Parks Middle School were all working hard to be good teachers. They genuinely wanted to help students learn and overcome their positions of poverty. But being good, taking on that identity, is a complicated thing. Theory for identity construction is important to understanding the ways in which teachers (and students, administrators, and consultants later in the book) negotiate the competing and conflicting narratives of Rosa Parks Middle School presented in the early chapters of this book as they make bids to be good.

Gee (2011) offers an alternative understanding of identity as something we perform through social interactions within institutions and between people rather than as something we have. He defines identity as "being recognized as a certain 'kind of person,' in a given context" (p. 99). People have the agency, or as Holland et al. (1998) describe, a modicum of agency, to construct their identities within the confines of the institutional framework that inscribe structures on them (Foucault, 1977; Bettie, 2003; Holland et al., 1998). Bettie (2003) argues that while there is no essential self, the fixed nature of the identities constructed by the institution make people feel as though the "real self" temporarily constructed by the institution in a given moment is somehow who they really are. For example, when the institution of school constructs a student as at-risk, they come to see themselves as being at-risk in all they do. Thus, when people attempt to construct an identity that differs from that inscribed on them by an institution, they feel like they are pretending to be someone they are not, or "passing" in Bettie's words. This feeling of not really belonging brought on by the institutional identity is what reproduces class structures because people stay where they feel they belong, understanding that positioning as connected to an essential, unchangeable self.

Foucault's (1977) concept of the carceral society (the idea of social discipline and surveillance in modern society) explains how normalizing institutions—like schools—produce "Truths" about the normalcy of class positioning. Though teachers are often considered middle class, Samuel and Ronald mirror their working-class students through *code switching* (switching between standard English and the slang their students use). They are *membershipping* (working to create identities that match with those of the students' home lives) with these high-needs students. Samuel and Ronald are also expected to do as they are told. Creativity and critical thinking are not expected or welcome in the same way they are for teachers in neighboring affluent schools.

Samuel and Ronald's identities as teachers are being constructed in part by the normalizing institution of schooling in the United States through the narratives of urban schools and urban school reform in popular culture, and in popular culture's understanding of school, based on their jobs in a school serving a neighborhood of poor, minority people where violence often occurs. The normalizing narratives of the urban teacher identity within the testing and accountability narrative are highly regimented. Teachers are to uniformly follow the pacing guide provided by the district and keep the children quiet and under control. Teacher-proof programs like Achieve3000 reduce their jobs to policing students while the computer makes the assignments and does the grading. Outsiders who come into the school to fix what's wrong there also surround them. While the testing and accountability narrative expects teachers to act almost as robots, pop culture narratives are either those of the hero/martyr or the deadbeat teacher. There is no in-between. The hero/ martyr teacher is expected to connect with students and live their lives for those students and the school. Otherwise they are deadbeats who don't care about the students. The urban teacher must negotiate a balance between regimentation and being someone with whom the children will identify. In their bids to be good teachers, Samuel and Ronald had to negotiate with the urban teacher identity and how it tempers the ability to be a good teacher for educators like them. Gee (2011) labels this sort of identity construction as *institutional identity* or I-identity, where the power of construction is located in the institution. The institution determines what constitutes a good teacher.

But there is hope for change. Bettie (2003) argues that when people do attempt to "pass" in social situations where they feel they do not belong, they open up the possibility for change in the institutional structure. In order to pass, people must negotiate known narratives of how to be in a context with new ones. Holland et al. (1998) talk about this negotiation of narratives in terms of improvisation, where people "perform self" by bringing the lived narratives of their histories (the stories of their lives by which they define who they are in the world) into a new social situation. The students and teachers in the narratives in this book are not new to the school, the community, or to writing, but they are new to the narrative of writing that the Writing Project brought and the accompanying writing assignments. The teachers and students then had to improvise in order to perform good teacher and good student identities in these new social situations. Holland et al. point to improvisation as having transformative potential. Improvisation opens up space, much like Bettie's concept of "passing," for change.

Over time, the improvisations of earlier generations can become the expectations of the next, espousing change. Gee (2011) refers to this passing and improvisation, or these newly negotiated identities, as *discourse identity* or D-identity. The negotiation of narratives must be recognizable by others in order for it to be an identity, so the power for identity construction lies in discourse or dialogue with other individuals. These identities are not distinct from institutional identities, and so institutions certainly make use of discourse identities in order to solidify the institution's social hegemonic position. For this reason, improvisation does not guarantee change or transformation; it simply has the potential for it because we are constantly making and remaking scenes in our daily lives. In the cases of Samuel and Ronald, the institutional identity of urban teacher is inscribed upon them. I will examine how Samuel's discourse identity complies with the urban teacher identity of doing as he is told in his bid for a good teacher identity. The urban teacher identity matches with the narrative of his lived history about how to be a teacher. Ronald's discourse identity contains a performance of resistance to the urban teacher identity as he complies with the ideas of the writing consultants, who bring a different narrative of good teacher as a creative, critical thinker. In his discourse identity, Ronald is negotiating these narratives along with his lived history of how to be a writer and a writing teacher.

COMPETING NARRATIVES OF WRITING

The school's adoption of the computerized literacy program Achieve3000 in the third year of their partnership with the Writing Project is indicative of the competing narratives of writing instruction in the world of Rosa Parks Middle School. If we consider writing itself as a mediating tool in the activity of knowledge-making and sharing, an analysis of Achieve3000 (itself a mediating tool for writing instruction) can help illuminate the conflicting narratives of writing that students and teachers at Rosa Parks Middle School had to negotiate.

Achieve3000 was a highly efficient literacy producing and monitoring software program approved for school purchase by the state and encouraged in schools bearing low performing status. At Rosa Parks Middle School, each student spent 45 minutes, or half of each English/language arts class, in the computer lab working with an article assigned by the computer program. Students silently read and answered multiple-choice questions and filled in the blanks when prompted with information from the article in order to complete an essay. The computer then scored the essays and sent the report to the teacher, administrators, and the district office.

The teacher's role in this activity was to monitor the students while they worked. Teachers were to walk up and down the line of computers, checking to see that the students were on task. They were also to monitor the reports that the program creates for each student. Administrators access the reports to monitor the teachers. They informed the teachers that Achieve3000 time was not to be used to converse with colleagues, grade papers, plan lessons, or even to conference with students about their writing or their ideas.

When we first came to Rosa Parks Middle School, we learned that writing in this world was to follow a rigid form, and that form was to be filled in with the right ideas as decided by the teachers, who were themselves being monitored by the administrators, the district, the state, and the testing industry. With the addition of Achieve3000, the software corporation had great power in deciding what ideas were right and how they fit together. English/language arts teachers therefore felt that their time for writing instruction was full and did not take up any of the ideas that we offered as writing consultants.

When we left the school at the end of our three-year study, the dominant narrative of writing in the figured world of the school was that students do not do it when asked, and that the structured testing and accountability narrative of writing is something that they need in order to be prepared for the rigors of tests they will take in high school if they are to go to college. Within this narrative, the state determines that students should write in all subject areas, but it does not define that writing. The software corporation determines what non-fiction information students read and write about and how they write about it.

The narrative of writing in our figured world, as Writing Project consultants brought in to help, was in conflict with the intersecting figured worlds of the testing industry, software corporation, schooling in the United States, and urban school reform. We viewed writing as a mediating tool, not an outcome in and of itself. In our narrative, writing was about the sharing of ideas, critically and creatively thinking, and bringing forward new ideas. In our view it was a mediating tool that can connect students' daily lives to the information they learn in school, and a mediating tool with which to inquire into legitimizing power structures. Our narrative of writing then was in conflict with that of many other narratives of writing constructing the school world. And yet we also slid into a commodified narrative of writing as well, asking teachers to do our "thing" of using daybooks and allowing students to think critically and creatively through writing. When teachers and administrators constructed us as "do-gooders," we, in turn, constructed teachers and administrators as simply not getting "it"—the narrative that the Writing Project was promoting.

There are narratives of writing at work in the world of Rosa Parks Middle School that critique the dominant testing and accountability narrative of writing. They exist in what the teachers are doing in their classrooms behind closed doors, what the students are doing in their writing in and out of school, and even in the ideas of writing that we, as outside consultants, were attempting to put forward. However, students whose thoughts in writing did not fit into the school world's socializing narrative of right were constructed as problematic, as will be seen in the following chapters where students' Holocaust diary writings caused concern due to their "inappropriate" content. The students were aware of what counted as school writing, as is noticeable in their interviews as well as in the differences in the various narratives that appeared in their school essay writing assignments and the other forms they engaged with in and out of school. I will examine these writings in much more detail in Chapters 4 and 5.

DIARY WRITING: A NARRATIVE OF CONVERGENCE

Let's return to the vignette that opened this chapter where students read diary entries in which they imagined living during the Holocaust. I went to the school to collect the students' diaries because the academic facilitator and Samuel wanted me to look at them closely and think about ways to publish them. They also wanted me to know that this was the first time all year that all of the students had actually done their homework or been engaged in schoolwork.

The academic facilitator read Erin's entry out loud, beaming and crying at the power of the student's writing. As I sorted through the other papers and asked about other classes who did the same assignment, she explained that they had a "problem" because some of the entries weren't "appropriate for school" and most of them were rife with grammatical errors.

I met with Samuel the following week to talk more about the diary entries and the assignment. In that interview and in subsequent conversations with him about this moment in his classroom, he said that this was his best day in nine years of teaching. He told me the story of how he got to the diary assignment. He had been teaching a unit on World War II, and in order to explain how the Holocaust could have happened, he made Adolph Hitler, in his words, "look like a good guy" in order to help the students see how Germans and others living at the time could be drawn to someone or something we so clearly see now as wrong. He worried that he had been too convincing and that the students were getting the "wrong" message, so he showed the film *Remembering the Holocaust: Children's Diaries* to make sure they got the "right" message about the atrocities of Hitler's regime. He got the idea to have them write the diaries from our workshop on using different genres/forms with course content.

The film was narrated with sad tones and music, describing diary passages from children during the Holocaust, with images of the atrocities and from the war.

We sat with the stack of papers. He pulled out the ones he most wanted me to see and shuffled others to the bottom of the pile, saying that these students had mishandled the assignment and their entries weren't worth my time. He shared the academic facilitator's concerns about the school appropriateness of some of the work and the errors in the conventions of writing. The "inappropriate" pieces had veered from a retelling of the film narrative to include more of the writer's ideas and personal histories. I will look at one of these in detail in Chapter 6.

Samuel had never tried this sort of informal writing and was thrilled with the results overall. He wanted to publish the students' work in some way to keep it with him and to remind him of the success. He wanted my help because he said that he was not comfortable with his ability to "teach writing." He had given the assignment because he knew that he was now required to teach some writing in his class. The district central office and the state had begun to require writing in all subject areas in order to support the CCSS in English/ language arts, but the district and state were not specific about what that writing should look like, other than that it should be connected to the material the students were studying. Samuel did not know what to do next with the diary writing, but he did know he wanted to do something significant with it. I explained that while wonderful, these pieces were first drafts and had great potential for working through multiple drafts because the students were so engaged with the writing and proud of it. He was concerned that he did not have any more time to work closely with the pieces in class because he had to move on with the other content he needed to teach. The standards that he was required to teach focused on content, not writing; therefore, extended time spent on a writing assignment, no matter how engaging and powerful, did not make sense to him in his compliance with the expectations of the school district and the administrators.

Tallulah and I ultimately decided to make a video recording of the students reading selections from their diaries, since it was the act of the reading of them out loud in class that seemed to be the significant moment. We also asked the girls to reflect on the experience as a part of the video. We then edited the readings and interviews together into a movie. I conducted formal interviews with several of the students, and I examine some of those in Chapters 5 and 6.

In his negotiation of the narratives of the figured world of Rosa Parks Middle School, Samuel's discourse identity is in compliance with the institutional identity of "urban hero teacher." He is committed to both the students and to following the rules of the institution. Samuel is an African American male with a close haircut. He typically wears a Rosa Parks

Middle School polo shirt and khakis to work, emulating the uniform the students wear. He is also a football coach, and his appearance works with his coaching identity. Samuel is known for strict discipline in his classroom. The students move around the classroom in an orderly way, getting books from the shelves in an orderly, silent manner, or being sent back to their seats to start over if they do not comply. The same rules apply for lining up to leave. However, he also memberships with the students by code-switching and giving them nicknames. He jokes with them individually as they enter and exit the classroom. One day when I was observing, he was ragging a 6th grader about his height, saying "Dude, why you so short? When you gonna grow?" While in some cultures this may seem terribly insulting to the child, it mimics the way these students talk to and kid with one another. It is emblematic of the camaraderie between Samuel and the students.

Samuel keeps an orderly classroom, is orderly in his appearance, works hard to be someone the students respect and identify with, and gives extra time to coaching after a long day of teaching. He works to follow the rules by giving the writing assignment suggested by the consultants in compliance with the school system mandate that he put more writing into his lessons, even though he is very uncomfortable with his own ability to teach writing.

As I mentioned before, the diary assignment complies with the testing and accountability narrative wherein learning is "doing what one is supposed to do." Samuel is teaching writing in social studies because the state and district say he must do it, the administrator is watching to be sure he does it, and we as consultants are watching to make sure he does it in a way that we wanted. Samuel, the academic facilitator, and the consultants said the students were engaged because they all did their homework—what they were supposed to do. We published the student work in a movie that was shown to the administrators to show that the students are doing good work so we have succeeded in doing what we were supposed to do: getting writing into the school in content areas. In this convergent narrative there is no room for movement or change. Any movement away from giving back exactly what the consultants said to do in terms of assignment making, or away from the narrative of the film in terms of what the students were writing is viewed as deviant behavior. There is no space here for pushing at the boundaries and creating something new and different. The narrative solidifies Samuel in his position of working-class, urban teacher who does as he is told and does not veer from that. Even the way the academic facilitator and Samuel respond to the students who didn't simply retell the narrative of the film falls into this narrative of convergence. Here, learning is giving back what you have been told.

The Holocaust diary assignment came to be the narrative by which the students, and in some ways Ronald, the second teacher in this chapter, defined the type of writing in which the Writing Project was interested. More than a year after the initial assignment in Samuel's class, when I interviewed the students in Ronald's class about writing in social studies, they began by referring back to these Holocaust diaries. This assignment was the reference point by which the students described not only their writing in social studies class the following year, but all of their school writing in their conversations with me. So in many ways, this moment of writing that we were all so excited about became a closed circuit. Samuel did not go on to do any other writing assignments in his classroom. In fact, he left the classroom at the end of the year to become the dean of students, a position that deals predominantly with discipline. The students had this one moment to harken back to as a moment when they wrote, but as will be discussed in the following chapter, they did not equate it with the "real" writing they did in English class, which was the argument writing they did with Achieve3000. The students who were celebrated as successful in this assignment retold the narrative of the film without question or critique. Those who did question the narrative were seen as unsuccessful. Chapter 6 looks closely at one example of a student who was pushing at the boundaries of the film narrative and was considered unsuccessful. So while this moment lived in the minds of the teachers and students in the school as an example of student engagement and a time where students felt they were writers, it did nothing to change the culture of writing in the school or the construction of students as writers, because the testing and accountability narrative of what writing should be had more power.

DAYBOOK WRITING: NARRATIVES OF RESISTANCE AND COMPLIANCE

I was at Rosa Parks Middle School one afternoon in early December in the third year of our work there to finish up a formal interview with Ronald about how he saw himself using writing in his social studies class. The Writing Project had given Ronald 170 composition books for his classes to use as daybooks. As I described in Chapter 2, the daybook is a tool for writing and thinking that the Writing Project brought to Rosa Parks Middle School in the first year of our partnership with them. Tallulah and I, along with other colleagues in the Writing Project, use this tool with our students as a place for getting ideas onto the page. The daybook is essentially a container for messy, on-the-spot thinking thrown on the page to be mined later for larger, more public pieces of writing. The daybook functions as a writer's notebook for students (Brannon et al., 2008). In our Writing Project site it functions as a way to record their thinking about the content of a class, the ways it might connect with their daily lives, and ideally, it allows them to begin to question the legitimizing power structures that are present. However, as I mentioned in Chapter 3, this empty composition book had become commodified. Having students write their thoughts and think about content in forms like acrostic poems or diary entries was the "thing" we had told the teachers to do. Ronald's interest in using the daybook was one of the main reasons I chose to study his classes.

When I checked into the office, I learned that he was in a new teachers' meeting being held by the district. I slipped into the back of the media center to wait for the meeting to end, and he came hurrying back. Breathlessly he said, "You'll never believe what the kids are doing," and then he was off, whispering away about what his students were writing, and ignoring the woman up front who was pointing to a PowerPoint slide and talking to the group of teachers who were also whispering among themselves, texting, or grading papers.

"Let's get out of here! I've got to show you this stuff!" Ronald grabbed my bags and hustled me out of the media center. He continued to talk, hands and bags waving, as we nearly ran down the hall. He started pulling out daybooks as soon as we got to his classroom, and said "Oh yes! Please!" when I interrupted to ask if I could turn on my recorder. For the next 30 minutes, he read to me from his students' daybooks, repeatedly saying how smart they were and how excited he was about what was happening in his classroom. He couldn't stop reading to me from the notebooks and telling me about the amazing discussions and deep understandings of social studies that were resulting from the writing. He had asked them to write from the prompt "I was standing by a pool of water and I saw . . ." He was excited about the descriptions the students gave and the insights he was able to glean about their lives from what they choose to write about. He was excited about the way he could use those insights to connect with them over the social studies content they were learning. He had also done a lesson using a CNN newscast to teach about nuclear weapons in Korea, and the students had done a quick-write that led to a lively discussion about war and the possibility of the draft.

He talked about how the students were getting so excited in the discussions that they were talking over one another—not usually condoned the school's orderly culture in which they were meant to speak after raising hands—but he hated to stop them because they were so engaged and enthusiastic. He talked about how he couldn't wait to work with his 7th graders to take what they had been doing with quick-writes in their daybooks and class discussions and move them into longer essays, particularly document-based questions. I felt like I was looking at the work of a master teacher. His classroom management style and the daybook assignments complied with my narrative of good teacher.

But then, as I was leaving he said, "You know, all of this is totally under the radar. No one even looked at these notebooks for my eval. and I got 'emerging teacher.' Whatever, I know I have a lot to learn." Here he was referring to his yearly evaluation required by the district and conducted by a school administrator in which he was not considered to be an exemplary teacher but rather a novice who didn't quite know what he was doing. The notebooks and the discussions that I held in such high esteem and that he was so proud of were meaningless to his evaluators, who were looking for evidence of compliance with the testing and accountability narrative of order and control. His improvisation evident in his discourse identity of good teacher was not recognizable by the school even as it was recognizable to me, the writing consultant. Neither of the assignments we were looking at was on the pacing guide and therefore held no value in his evaluation.

Three months later, I slipped into the end of Ronald's first two-hour block. The lights were low, and 32 pencils in the hands of 32 students were scribbling as fast as they could go. Some students were squashed together, bumping elbows at a back table because there weren't enough desks. They didn't notice each other, or me, when I walked into the room. Ronald called time, and some began to put away their notebooks and get in line, but others were still writing. One child walked over to me and whispered, "Were you here? Did you see how brilliant we were? Did you get that in your notes?" As I sat staring at the child in stunned silence, kicking myself for being late getting out the door that morning, Ronald opened the door to lead the students to their next class and bellowed down the hall, "We've got some writers up in here!" The students gathered their things and slowly followed him out, grinning, talking, and pushing each other until they got to the hall where strict silence and order was enforced.

Ronald was nearly dancing when he came back in, once again grabbing notebooks and this time reading the acrostic poems the students had written based on a gallery crawl of images from the slave trade that he had posted around the room. He prided himself in representing two sides of every story, and the images depicted slaves piled onto ships as well as slave owners and slave boat captains. The students were to write from all of those points of view. In the entries he read to me, he valued critical thinking over simple retelling. For the most part he was thrilled simply that all the students had written. For Ronald, learning was about thinking rather than retelling the narrative given by the teacher. He was, though, compliant with our view of teaching and learning. He was "passing" as a teacher in a middle-class school where creativity and critical thinking on the part of teachers and students is valued, although he was working in a school where those values were not sought.

Other teachers on Ronald's team came in to see what all of the excitement was about, and they began to marvel with him about the outstanding thinking and writing the students had done. This out-of-meeting sharing among teachers was rebellious in and of itself, and when someone mentioned telling the administration about it a hush fell over the room. The other 7th-grade teacher had done a different activity in her class, and the school policy was to follow the same curriculum in all classes. If Ronald "told," they would both be "in trouble." They would be reprimanded for not following the same curriculum, and this was particularly dangerous as the principal had strategic staffing power, meaning that she could replace non-compliant teachers. The testing and accountability narrative of the school was that all students should be doing the same thing, following the pacing guide, at all times. Ronald had disregarded the policy, and that mattered more in the world of the school than the kind of thinking and learning that was taking place in Ronald's classroom.

Ronald's classroom was much different from Samuel's. It was often noisy as students shared what they are thinking with partners and groups and talked to one another while moving around the room, but it was a purposeful noise. He embraced the workshop approach we brought from the Writing Project and resisted the order and control of the larger testing and accountability narrative. Ronald is an African American male with dreadlocks that he wears neatly tied back. He also often has a beard in different stages of growth, from full beard to goatee. Most days, he wears dress slacks, a long-sleeved button-down shirt, and a tie. However, like Samuel he embraces the hero teacher identity, membershipping with the kids by code-switching and coaching track in his afterschool hours. Ronald self identifies as a writer and is comfortable with the identity of writing teacher within the social studies courses that he teaches.

In many ways, the narrative of Ronald and his daybook activities is a narrative of compliance as well as resistance. In some ways, Ronald was negotiating a discourse identity of resistant teacher. He resisted the institutional identity inscribed on him by the institution's narrative of the urban teacher who follows directions and keeps order and control above all else. He ducks out of meetings, brushes off the fact that the writing his students are doing doesn't count in his evaluation, and resists the idea of teaching exactly the same thing at the same time as his colleagues. He allows his classroom to be a noisy, bustling place where kids write what they think rather than regurgitating the narrative he gives them, and where they talk over one another in their excitement to share those thoughts. And yet, in resisting the administrator's directives, Ronald was compliant with the Writing Project narrative by using the daybook. In his discourse and dialogue with me, he is recognizable as a brilliant teacher who excites his students about learning and gets them to think through writing, but in the world of the school, because of his institutional identity of urban teacher, he is recognized as resistant and a problematic teacher even while being recognized as a hero/martyr teacher because of his relationship with the students and the extra time he gives to coaching.

NEGOTIATING GOOD TEACHER IDENTITIES IN A COMPLEX WORLD

Both Samuel and Ronald were negotiating how to be teachers within the figured world of Rosa Parks Middle School. They both enacted good urban teacher discourse identities, but in different ways. While Ronald improvised more resistance than Samuel by not complying with the administration in terms of keeping a quiet classroom, following the pacing and curriculum guide, and attending all of the new teachers' meeting, he was still in compliance with what the Writing Project consultants wanted him to do. Both men enacted hero teacher by committing extra time to the school through coaching and working hard to have good relationships with the students.

Teaching in an urban school is incredibly complex. Teachers must negotiate the testing and accountability narrative of regimented order and control while working to identify with and engage their students. There are also often outsiders coming in to fix what's wrong. As Writing Project consultants, we brought an outside narrative of teaching and learning to the school that valued creativity and critical thinking on the part of the teachers and the students. This narrative is more often recognizable in middle-class schools, but not in low-income settings. Teachers have to improvise how to be good teachers within that competing urban school reform narrative of schooling.

Samuel attempts to pass as a writing teacher by using the assignment given to him in a faculty meeting by the Writing Project. He relies on the administration and the consultants to tell him what to do next with this writing, which he considers remarkable though problematic. In this way Samuel reproduces the socialization process of the school. He retains the identity of working-class teacher doing as he is told and is considered to be a very successful teacher in the school. He was promoted the year after the Holocaust diaries to become dean of students, though it is significant that this appointment carried no curriculum duties, and certainly not writing instruction duties.

Ronald saw himself as a writer and was therefore more comfortable with the writing teacher narrative brought to the school by the Writing Project. In some ways, his enactment of good teacher resists and critiques the urban teacher narrative that says do as you are told because he resists the narrative of order and control and the narrative of learning as retelling information. However, in his compliance with the Writing Project narrative of teaching and learning that critiques the urban narrative, Ronald attempted to pass as a middle-class teacher. Therefore, he is labeled as emergent teacher—a teacher with a lot to learn, or a problematic teacher. Ronald left the school at the end of the following year for a position at a charter school where his ideas and ways of being teacher were more respected.

5:

REPRODUCING "GOOD STUDENT" WRITING

One day in May of our third year at Rosa Parks Middle School, I met for lunch with a group of students who had agreed to be interviewed. The students, from Ronald's honors class, were the only ones who agreed to participate. Out of the class of 28, only 4 students returned the form to be interviewed. The other students were shy or perhaps a bit suspicious of me as an adult outsider and while willing to let me observe class were not comfortable with interviews. I interviewed the students as a group and videotaped the interview. Figure 5.1 shows my interview questions.

FIGURE 5.1. STUDENT INTERVIEW QUESTIONS

1. Tell me about writing in this class.
2. Tell me about writing in other classes at school.
3. Tell me about a piece of writing that you are really proud of.
4. Do you do any writing outside of school?
5. Where did you go to elementary school?
6. Where do you live now?
7. Is there anything else you would like to tell me about your writing?

The students were happy to talk and very polite (and appreciative of the pizza and fruit provided). As we began the interview and I asked them about what kind of writing they did in social studies class, they each identified themselves by whether they had been in Samuel's class the year before during the now-famous Holocaust diary assignment. To them, the assignment and experience was a significant part of writing in social studies. They went on to talk about how they used daybooks in Ronald's class. These students felt that they knew what I was interested in, and as good students, they complied and talked about it.

In this chapter and the next, I look more closely at the writing of the four students that I interviewed. They all happen to be girls for two reasons. First, Samuel's class that experienced the Holocaust diary writing moment was an all-girls class. Second, of the students I interviewed, only the girls shared their daybooks with me. There is something interesting here at work about why the boys either didn't buy into daybook writing or didn't trust me to look at it. Other scholars have written about girls having an easier time enacting good student in school by giving back what the teacher has told them (Freudenthaler, Spinath, & Neubauer, 2008; Van Houtte, 2004; Wong, Lam, & Ho, 2002; Bulcock, Whitt, & Beebe, 1991; Epstein, Elwood, Jey & Maw, 1998). The fact that these were all students in a low-performing school where the institutional identity of "student" required just that (giving back what the teacher has told them) could explain why boys did not volunteer for the project. I did work with boys, even playing football with them in return for some writing they did in class for me, but I was not able to build the relationships needed for them to return the permissions form that would allow me to study their writing or interview them.

The Holocaust diary assignment was a marked moment in our work at Rosa Parks Middle School. It was embraced by all parties working with the students (consultants, principal, and teachers) and by the students as well. It was a moment that was referenced over and over again in our discussions with teachers and students, and in many ways, it was a moment that was never repeated again. Ronald's classes did take up the daybook and extend on the moment by doing similar assignments and extending those assignments to more formal writing, but his classes were the only ones to do so.

To complete the Holocaust diary assignment, students had to negotiate narratives about the Holocaust from the film and their teacher, the multiple intersecting narratives of knowledge and writing at Rosa Parks Middle School, and non-school narratives from their lives to create a *theory-in-use* (the theory they are using about how the world works) about how to do this assignment. Later, when sharing their diaries in class and during interviews with me, they had to reimagine and negotiate these scenes while hearing the sound of their voices and feeling the eyes of their peers, their teacher, their principal, and the consultants on them. To complete the daybook assignments in Ronald's class, students were required to go through many of the same negotiations. I will look closely at the students' writing and their words about their writing in order to examine in an in-depth way the ideas of compliance and resistance in the student role.

In this chapter I examine how three of these students were negotiating competing narratives of writing and how to be a good student at Rosa Parks Middle School. Two of the students shared daybook entries from Ronald's class, while one shared both her Holocaust diary from Samuel's class and her daybook. Each student and her writing produced different material realities.

The girls perform good student as defined by the institution's construction of them as good at-risk students, in that for each of them, in the figured world of Rosa Parks Middle School, being a good student means repeating back what they've been told by the adults or the text. In the United States' pop-culture model, the narrative of a successful person is one of innovation and creativity. Value is placed on the creativity and thinking of people such as Steve Jobs and Mark Zuckerberg. However, in this school serving lower-income cultural groups, people are expected to follow orders, do as they are told, and take all information given to them by a person of authority as "Truth." When the girls negotiate the various narratives of the school along with their lived histories in order to improvise in this new narrative of writing and new social situation of talking with the university writing consultant, they improvise by harkening back to the Holocaust diary, the assignment they know I was excited about. However, the at-risk institutional identity heavily inscribed the construction and performance of the good-student discourse identity. The Holocaust diary entries that Samuel and the academic facilitator considered to be successful repeated the narrative of the film that the students watched without critiquing it or creating other narratives. They gave back what they were given. In the analysis below, I will look at the way in which the narrative of urban school reform as inscribed on these three girls socializes them in a way that potentially reproduces their socioeconomic positioning.

CRITICAL DISCOURSE ANALYSIS:
A MICRO ANALYSIS OF LANGUAGE AND IDENTITY

In this chapter as well as the chapter that follows, I use Gee's *critical discourse analysis* (CDA) along with Gee's categories of identity (discourse identity and institutional identity) in order to examine how each student's language about their writing is constructing and performing the roles of "good at-risk student" or "bad at-risk student" in different ways as the students improvise in the new social and writing situations in which they find themselves.

I am using James Paul Gee's (2010) critical discourse analysis because of his understanding of situated language and what the language is doing within a figured world and the activity of that figured world. For Gee, people function in the world by living their theories-in-use, constructing narrative worlds in which they operate. By using Gee's CDA, I am able to analyze the various, often competing and conflicting narratives that students negotiate as they sit down to write and how their language about writing is building the figured world of Rosa Parks Middle School. Such microanalysis illustrates the supremely complex nature of writing in a low-performing urban school as well as the socializing nature of writing at Rosa Parks Middle School. Because CDA is a microanalysis tool, I will be looking at very short snippets of language situated within the larger context of the interviews. For a full explanation of Gee's CDA, see Appendix A. Also, each interview is broken down into stanzas in the appendix in order to further isolate the language and examine what it is constructing.

LESLIE: GOOD STUDENT WRITERS REPEAT

Leslie was a 7th-grade student in Ronald's honors social studies class. She was admired by all of her teachers and was at the top of her class in GPA. Her negotiations of the various narratives of the school, her discourse identity, embodies her good at-risk student institutional identity as inscribed on her by the narrative of urban school reform. Leslie wears the school uniform, including the argyle shirt, in the clean, pressed form reminiscent of retail management; she is performing good student as designed by the school board and department store. Her hair is neatly and carefully braided, also performing the neat, clean-cut expectation of the retail management business narrative. Orderliness, control, and uniformity are inscribed on her body in the way she carefully follows the school's uniform policy with no deviations.

Leslie's activities outside of school are also orderly and controlled. She explained that she had no free time, and that her life consisted of going to school, doing her homework, and traveling to her activities such as soccer, church, and music lessons at a local private college. The urban school reform narrative views unstructured after-school time as one of the things that lead to crime and poverty for students in low-income neighborhoods like Leslie's. Leslie is performing good at-risk student by keeping her time structured. When asked about why she participates in so many activities, Leslie explained that she intended to go to college, and these activities are necessary if she is to get a scholarship, which she needed because her family couldn't afford tuition. Leslie did not question how these activities would get her to college, or if other activities might serve her in the same way. She and her family did what the school—the castle on the hill—told her will make her successful without really questioning what the institution means by success.

In her writing, Leslie evokes the narrative of school learning in which good students give back the information presented to them by their teachers. Giving back is what the urban reform narrative expects of good at-risk students, as is illustrated by the dominant narrative of learning in the testing and accountability narrative, and specifically the Achieve3000 narrative of writing, in which students fill in the blanks of an essay form with words from the article they are given. Leslie's daybook is filled with careful, neat writing and every assignment is completed. In her daybook, giving back with order and control is just as apparent in her writing about her personal life as it is in her writing about the content of social studies. For example, in the journal entry below she agreed with the class motto "Work hard and be successful" and writes about studying in order to get a 100 on the unit test:

1. What score do you want to make on the unit 1 test?
   I want to make 100 on the unit 1 test.

2. What did you do to ensure that you reach your goal?
   Study and make sure you understand the questions they are asking, that's how you/I can reach your/my goal.

Leslie negotiated the conflicting narratives of writing in the school world to perform a discourse identity that matched the institutional identity inscribed on her, repeating back what she's been told: that hard work and doing well on a test will bring her success. She wrote that she wants to make a 100, *ventriloquating* (Bakhtin, 1981) or speaking through another's voice, in this case her teacher's, the trope of perfection. She adds that she will do that by studying and "understanding the questions they are asking." She did not say what she would study. She places the onus on the questions and understanding them. If she can understand the questions, she can answer them by giving back what they are asking her for. Her construction of "you/I" and "your/my" is intriguing because she is both claiming her power in what to do and distancing herself from it at the same time. On the one hand she was claiming her power to do these things using "I," but on the other she was saying that's what "you" need to do, mimicking a teacher talking to students. In her writing she was saying that if you study something (she doesn't say what) and understand the questions, you will be successful. There is no room for critiquing or questioning those questions. It's the person's fault for not working hard enough (studying) if she doesn't understand, and success is defined as making a 100 on the test, which harkens back to the testing and accountability narrative.

In this response there was a third prompt asking about the content of the social studies class.

3. How were civilizations developed through human-environment interaction?
   The civilizations develop through human-environment interaction by just using your environment /or like we said "interacting."

In her writing about the content of social studies, Leslie relies on the words in the question to answer the question. Her answer doesn't explain what human-environment interaction is or what it might have to do with civilization. She simply repeats back the text of the question, filling in the blanks with information given to her in the text, much like the Achieve3000 program asks the students to do. Presumably, her teacher has given a real answer to this question, but she doesn't produce that answer. Her teacher, who does not call her out on this non-answer, considers her good-student identity of repeating back good enough. In the figured world of Rosa Parks Middle School, this is the response that marks a person as a good student. In the narrative of urban school reform, it marks her as good at-risk student.

Leslie's negotiations of the various narratives of Rosa Parks Middle School as she works to enact good student in a group interview about writing in Ronald's class solidify her institutional identity as at-risk. Being interviewed by the writing consultant who is a university researcher is a new situation for Leslie. In order to participate in the interview, Leslie must improvise, drawing on her known experiences in order to decide how to perform. She is negotiating several narratives. She negotiated the urban school reform narrative and the testing and accountability narrative of writing along with the order and control narrative in the school. In addition, she was negotiating the new, conflicting narrative of writing that was brought by the writing consultant, in which writing was used to explore ideas and think about things on paper through informal writing in composition books called "daybooks." The consultant's narrative was something new and different that the students were doing in social studies. In the improvisation below, Leslie continued to perform the good at-risk student in that she repeats what Ronald told the students about the new daybook writing on a day I observed in class, blending the new experience with the narrative of orderly, controlled reading and writing in the school. She also constructs writing as a commodity that will help students, ventriloquizing the urban reform narrative of literacy.

In response to my question "Can you tell me a little bit about writing in general in this class?", she says:

> Writing, uh, helps you organize your thoughts and how you felt towards a certain subject or topic. And it helps you understand the text or what you are reading better, but writing, writing's good.

In this articulation, Leslie spoke through the urban reform narrative by offering writing as a thing to do that will solve a problem and by presenting writing as a separate activity from reading. Her narrative commodified writing by making it a thing that "you" need in order to be organized and to help "you" understand the things "you" read in school. She also constructed the writing in social studies as different, negotiating what she understood as the different narrative of writing that I, the writing consultant who is interviewing her, had brought into the figured world of Rosa Parks Middle School. In Leslie's narrative of writing, if "you" write, "you" will be organized and understand reading in "certain" instances. Writing is the commodity that does that for "you."

Throughout the transcript, Leslie distanced herself from the activity of writing in social studies class by using the words *you* and *your* rather than *I* or *we*. Through this distancing she enacted teacher, mimicking Ronald and offering writing as a solution to the problem of understanding. She constructs writing as a thing, a commodity, by placing *writing* in the subject position in the sentence "Writing, uh, helps you organize your thoughts and how you felt towards a certain topic." Here, *writing* has the power, rather than *you,* the person performing the act of writing. Writing is the thing that organizes your thoughts and feelings. Without it, you are disorganized in your thinking and feeling, so you need writing. Or at least you need it in certain situations. She used the adjective *certain* in order to describe *subjects.* She did not say that writing does this for all subjects or topics, but she did not say which "certain topic[s]." Her use of the term *certain* signaled a difference between writing in social studies, what I've asked her about, and writing in other situations. She constructed a difference in the writing consultant's narrative of writing and the dominant narrative of writing in the school.

Leslie then said "It helps you understand the text or what you are reading better." Here, her language signals a shift to language that a reading specialist might use. She continued to build her argument for writing by offering writing as a tool to help "you understand" "text or what you are reading" and again mimicked Ronald, who I observed using similar words to explain daybook writing to the class. Her language constructs a difference between reading and writing, in that reading requires actions by you to be helpful. *You* appears in the subject position ("Reading helps you understand . . .), constructing writing as a tool that you can use in order to understand. Writing here becomes something that must be used in order to produce results. Writing on its own can "organize" thoughts and feelings, but in order to help with reading, you must use it. This necessity of a *you* to do something also appears in the way "text" is constructed as different from "what you are reading" by her use of the word "or." The text is just there and can be understood by writing.

In the world that Leslie's language builds, writing about a text, whether the student has read it or not, can help with understanding, while reading requires action in addition to writing if "you" are going to "understand better," as she said. The word *better* constructs *you* as already understanding before writing about it, but when *you* write, *you* add to your understanding. Writing is therefore necessary for better understanding. She evokes the testing and accountability narrative of schooling that says reading is about understanding. This understanding of reading is socializing Leslie and is potentially reproductive, because in the same way that students are to take what teachers say and give it back in writing, they are to do so with reading. They are not to critique what they read and extend upon it, thinking deeply about it and how it works with other things they have read or know. They are simply to take it at face value as "Truth."

Finally, Leslie described writing as good when she said ". . . but writing, writing is good." She doesn't say how it's good, or what's good about it. It's just good and there is no reason to question its goodness. She began this argument about writing with the single word *writing* and ends it with placing writing in the subject position and then judging it as "good." Here, Leslie ends her argument by constructing her identity as good student because she writes in social studies and writing is "good."

The commodified narrative of writing that Leslie ventriloquated is socializing and potentially reproductive in that when the reform narrative tells children to write, the children do writing, and if they are still unorganized or fail to better understand what they are reading, then there must be something wrong with the student. Leslie doesn't question this narrative. She simply repeats it, much like her daybook answer above (though here she has given a more comprehensible answer that addresses the question she has been asked). She participates in extracurricular activities, just as the narrative of urban school reform tells her she must do. She does everything just as she's told, listens carefully and repeats back all of the information she is given, and trusts that this will get her to college. The institution is constructing her identity, and in doing so it is making it even more difficult for her to compete for university seats or for scholarships with the creative, innovative students in the upper-middle-class school down the road.

ERIN: GOOD STUDENTS TRY TO RECREATE SUCCESS

Erin was in Samuel's class as a 6th grader and in Ronald's class as a 7th grader. She was moved into the honors group after her 6th grade year. Erin's performance of self in school is quiet and shy. She wears the basic school uniform, typically a pleated khaki skirt and a plain blue shirt rather than the department store argyle. The orderliness of the school uniform is inscribed on her body, but she resisted this inscription with her almost too-big clothing and her soft hair, neatly brushed, worn loosely and covering her face, because it took away from the orderly intention of the uniform. She seemed to hide in the clothes and behind her hair. She said that her activities outside of school are centered around caring for her younger brother while her parents work and doing her homework. After the Holocaust diary experience, she started writing historical fiction based on movies that she saw and what she was learning in her social studies class in order to repeat the moment of attention and validation she had experienced. Like Leslie, her time was filled, but with the responsibility of childcare rather than a plethora of activities meant to get her to college. In this way, Erin's outside-of-school activity was recognizable in the institutional identity of at-risk student as inscribed by the narrative of urban school reform, in that she was working quite a bit of the time rather than attending enrichment activities. Ronald identifies Erin as a great writer, while Samuel and the academic facilitator were surprised by her success with the Holocaust diary the year before. As a 7th grader, her teachers describe her as a "good kid" who will "do well," and her overall GPA is a solid B.

For Erin, being a writer and a good student meant following the plot line of the historical narrative that her teacher had told her or that she saw in a film and not wavering from the way the narrative was presented. However, her performance of the roles of writer and good student did not include the daybook writing assignments or other writing assignments in school. In her negotiation of the various conflicting narratives of the school world, the other assignments did not carry the same value as the historical narratives. Her performance of self is that of a struggling student in other areas. Though her grades were good and her teachers saw her as a good student, she told me that 7th grade was hard because she didn't "understand decimals" in math. When I asked her about the document-based essay questions Ronald is working with in social studies she said, "it confuses me." She did not say anything else about it. She doesn't mention, beyond shrugging, writing in other classes. Her good-student identity has been constructed by the marked moment of the Holocaust diaries. It is there that she felt confident and identified as a good student, so she continued to replicate that experience over and over again. In other areas of school when she tried to enact good student, she felt like she was passing, in the words of Bettie (2003). She was not confident as good student in the context of the school and did not feel that she belonged in the honors classes. And so she hid behind her hair and her shyness, and in that way she negotiates a discourse identity of good student in the context of the school. Like Leslie, she repeated in order to enact good student, but rather than repeating what she was told by the teacher across subject areas, she clung to that one moment of success and repeated that.

Erin's Holocaust diary entry was showcased throughout the school. The complete diary entry can be found below:

Tuesday 7:23 am August 16, 1941

Dear Friend,

The day has come my 12th birthday the day that was suppose to be the happiest day of my life but it wasn't. My family and another family were hidden in a room behind a book shelf suddenly we heard a loud bang on the door. We were all quiet we could hear the terrifing whailing scream of children calling out for their mom but probibly their mom was gone. I tried to comfort my brother who was asking me why the other children were crying his question broke my heart I couldn't tell him the truth so I told him that he should go play with the other little boy from the other family who lived with us suddenly the 8th month old baby Julio started to cry his mom tried to quiet him so we wouldn't get caught but it was too later the Nazis found us as they walked in they pointed their rifles at us like if we were a hunting animal. As we walked to the consentration camp my brother was clapsed to me he wouldn't let go. When the nazi opened the fence he shoved us in we tripped. I got up to help my brother but I didn't see him off in the distance I saw my brother trying to get off the soldier, then my mom started screaming. Today my birthday was a horrible nightmare, suddenly a nazi officer came up to me screaming and pulled me away from my parents. I was dumbfounded he took me to a gigantic factory, he put me to cremate bodies suddenly my brothers body lay there angonizing with a bullet through his head blood still gushing out, in his hand was the small red toy car that I had given him for his birthday. As I took it from his hand he pressed my hand he was alive, but then he vanished I cried hard enough to make a river. As I took the car I though of all the memorable moments. Tears came to my eyes as I remembered all the happy family moments. Tears came to my eyes I did the job when I was done my brother was gone as I gave him my last good bye and a kiss on a cheek. I put him in the flaming fire I cried as I did this I whent back to my parents showed my mom the toy car and we started to cry I hope we got out soon but for now we have to live here until the Nazis get tire of us.

Erin's writing about finding her brother was moving for all in the room on the day she read it aloud. The scene she describes is quite graphic, but it also emulated the film the students watched, in which images of a crematorium are shown while a young girl narrates having to prepare the bodies. The camera then pans to a close-up of a small toy. In the film, another narrator mentioned that the day of her capture was her birthday and yet another narrated being torn from her family. Erin melds these images together in her writing. Writing in social studies, and writing an imagined diary in the class, were both new to Erin. She drew on her experience with school writing, giving back information, much like Leslie, and replicating the film narrative. She captured that narrative down to the behavior of a Holocaust survivor in the film and the image of the toy among the ashes. She received a good deal of acclaim for this improvisation, another new thing for Erin, and it became a marked moment for her in which she felt confident in her good student performance. The writing is rife with errors, but the teachers overlooked these in her read performance of the piece. The academic facilitator who shared the piece with me read it out loud as well. The oral reading of the piece was valued over the correctness in the writing, which contributed to Erin's new feelings of success.

I interviewed Erin one week after the Holocaust diary writing and reading event, and in response to my first question, "Tell me a little bit about yourself," she responded, "I like reading and sometimes I like to cry to get out of . . . to stop being angry." Erin's performance of self while interacting with the university writing consultant is bound up in the activity of crying, in that it is the second thing she tells me about herself. She cried as she read her holocaust diary, along with the other girls. Her diary entry also moved her teachers and classmates to tears, and she was noticed for that. Erin began her description of herself by performing reader, though not writer. She said "I like to read . . ." as she described herself. She then performed crier, when she said ". . . sometimes I like to cry . . ." Here she connected herself with the activity of crying in the classroom and the event I was interviewing her about, connecting my question about her to her involvement in the classroom event. She went on to construct crying as an activity that enables her to deal with anger when she said ". . . I like to cry to get out of . . . to stop being angry." In the world she's building, it is more acceptable to cry than it is to be angry. Anger is something she needs to "get out of."

Erin sees crying about the events of the Holocaust as acceptable and anger as unacceptable. Good students then cry; they don't get angry, even if the assignment calls for envisioning the death of one's brother. Here, Erin performs good at-risk student as inscribed on her by the institution of school, doing as she is told, not questioning the fact that one should simply cry and not get angry about envisioning the death of a brother.

After this event, Erin began to write from the perspective of young women in different historical contexts during her free time outside of school, sometimes orally sharing bits and pieces of that writing with Ronald, her 7th-grade social studies teacher, or with me. She was constructing and negotiating an achieved discourse identity of good student in that she was making a bid to be recognized in the world of the school as a good student, even though she didn't feel like a good student. In fact, she performs struggling student in other areas based on the narratives of her lived experience with the dominant testing and accountability narrative of school writing that she has encountered in these areas of school. Her stories were generally sad and overall followed the same structure as the original Holocaust narrative in that they take a moment from a historical context and retell the details through the eyes of a young woman.

In a second interview, one year after the Holocaust diary moment, I asked Erin about writing in Ronald's class. She responded first by telling me about writing she does at home that is quite similar to what she did with the Holocaust diaries, including watching a movie, *Titanic*, to get inspiration. She did not feel like a good student as the institution of school inscribed it on her, but she negotiated the urban reform narrative with that of the Holocaust diary experience, which she understood as the writing consultant narrative because the teachers had connected that moment with me, and she repeated that narrative over and over to her teachers and classmates as well as to me in order to be recognized as good student.

She had heard that good historical fiction is researched, and so she told me that she does this with her own stories. However, when asked about what she was finding, she said "nothing." Her bid for good student, like Leslie's, is socializing and potentially reproductive in that she repeats what's been given to her, without question, making her recognizable as a good at-risk student rather than good innovative student.

This second interview continued with the vast majority of Erin's answers coming in short bursts, carefully answering only what I've asked her and elaborating very little. However, when I made a second attempt to ask her about writing assignments in Ronald's class, she told me about a diary entry that she'd written for a unit on the West African slave trade. She enthusiastically tells me the entire story with no prompting:

> Umm, a girl, she was forced into marriage. She's from Morroco. Her name is Nina. Um, her parents died in an accident, so she has to take care of her three year old sister. And um she has to take her with her to the Sahara Desert, but she doesn't want to, because she's too small. But she ends up taking her and then um, uh, the people from Ghanauh they have a salt and gold trade, but they can't make it, so everybody's worried, because that's what they mainly trade, salt and gold. So, um, uh they start trading and she trades half of her live stock for water, and uh the other half, she wants to trade for diamonds, but there's a rumor going around that Egyptians are um, at night, they set up their tent to go to sleep and um, the Egyptians, go and um, they kill the parents and they take their little kids and they uh sell them as slaves.

Erin's retelling here has similar themes to her Holocaust diary. She has included details that were a part of the lesson that I observed in Ronald's class, particularly the difficult decisions about trading, mimicking details from what she's been told, as she did in the Holocaust diary assignment. Also similar to the Holocaust diary, the main character is taking care of a younger sibling after being forced away from her home, this time by a forced marriage rather than Nazi soldiers. In this story, the parents are dead rather than the sibling, and in the end, the children are sold into slavery rather than being imprisoned in a concentration camp. It is interesting that she tells me this story but never shows me the actual writing. It is oral, much like the Holocaust diary. She is much more comfortable with the oral telling or reading of her work than she is with her actual words on paper.

For Erin, performing the good student, particularly for me as an outsider, is about this one type of writing, even a year later. Her performance of good student was caught up in writing historical narratives that are researched inside and outside of class. However, when I looked in her daybook, the notebook that Ronald is using everyday in class and is so thrilled with (see Chapter 4) and the main teaching tool that I have been working with in the school, there was almost nothing there. She told me that she had another daybook at home that she would bring, but she never did. Toward the end of the interview, in an attempt to see more of her actual words on paper, I asked more about the daybook:

> C: Tell me a little bit about how you guys use this notebook [her daybook] in class.
>
> E: Umm sometimes, if it's Monday, he says to write about our weekend. Or if we had a spring break or something we have to write about what happened. We had a good time or not.
>
> C: Okay. What else do you write in there?
>
> E: Ummmm. We do a lot of writing in here. I don't really know where it is, but we had to umm either write a story or um just tell what it means. And this is what I wrote. [Looks through notebook and then closes it.]
>
> C: Alright. Is there anything else you want to tell me about your writing in class? Anything in particular I should look at when I start digging through your notebook?
>
> E: No.

Erin constructed the daybook as an activity in her performance of self in our interview. In the portions below, she started to talk about how the class uses the daybook to write about life, ventriloquating Ronald. However, when I signaled to her that I'm looking for another answer concerning the writing they do about the content of social studies, writing I've seen Ronald ask the students to do, she started to flounder, trying to negotiate what she perceived as what I wanted to hear. Feeling unsuccessful in this narrative, she ended our conversation, eventually telling me that there wasn't anything I should see in her daybook.

Erin constructed daybook writing as happening "sometimes" if it's a Monday, saying "Umm sometimes, if it's Monday, he says to write about our weekend. Or if we had a spring break or something we have to write about what happened. We had a good time or not." She says "he says to write," not "I write," or "we write," signifying that this was assigned, but she may or may not actually do it. She then explained an assignment about "Spring break or something" and said we "have to write, " emphasizing that writing is an obligation. Her words constructed daybook writing about "Spring break or something" as something she and the students in her class were compelled to do, not something she wanted to do or felt connected with. She does not mention writing about the content of the social studies class at all, connecting daybook writing in social studies only with things from life outside of school like breaks and weekends.

There is a shift in her approach when I signaled that her answer is not what I was looking for by answering "Okay" and asking "What else do you write in there?" without taking up anything she has previously said. Erin enacted searching for the right answer with "Ummmm" and a long pause. Then she constructed the daybook writing as a large part of what she and the other students do in class with her response "We do a lot of writing in here, I don't really know where it is, but we had to umm either write a story or um just tell what it means. And this is what I wrote." (Looks through notebook and then closes it.) However, when she acted as agent using *I* in the sentence "I don't know where it is," she used *it* to refer to writing, not stories, not words, but *it,* an unnamed thing. She then attempted to describe an assignment to me, still enacting compliant student, but her voice softened to barely audible and she seemed to sink back into her hair as she said "but we had to either write a story of um, just tell what it means." She pulled the daybook off of the desk between us onto her lap when she said "And this is what I wrote." She flipped through a few more pages and finally stopped speaking altogether and closed the notebook, keeping it in her lap, looking down with her hair completely covering her face. When I asked "Is there anything else you want to tell me about your writing in class? Anything in particular I should look at when I start digging through your notebook?" she constructed her daybook as not valuable to me by responding "No" to my question.

Erin's negotiation of the various narratives of school writing resulted in her bid to be recognized as a good student and to construct a good student discourse identity. These negotiations are bound up in the one activity with which she felt success. Her negotiation between the conflicting narratives of writing in the world of Rosa Parks Middle School led her to understand that good students repeat what is given to them, and that she was successful in both the new social situation and the "new" narrative of writing that was represented by the Holocaust diary. That success was recognized both by the dominant narrative of writing in the school and the new narrative of writing created by the writing consultants. However, she is uncomfortable in the role of good student as inscribed on her by the dominant narrative of school reform. She did not repeat back across the board in her schoolwork like Leslie; she simply continued to write in the exact style that brought her success over and over again. She stayed true to the orality of the experience by telling me the story instead of letting me read it. She enacted her discomfort with the good student label by hiding behind her hair, and she hid from my pressing questions about her daybook, finally hiding the writing itself from me.

For Erin, the diary and historical fiction writing has become the commodified thing that will bring her success. Like Leslie, she focused that activity around replicating and repeating the information she had been given, but she only saw her performances in historical fiction writing and diary writing as valuable in her performance of good student. She is not confident in other areas of social studies or writing, or even writing in social studies, and so she hides that writing, much in the way that she hides behind her hair, carefully negotiating narratives from her experiences outside of school that tell her to hide when she's not confident, with those of the school world that say good students show adults their work. Her performance was recognizable enough in the school world to construct her as good at-risk student deserving of being in the honors classes. However, it is socializing and potentially reproductive because in her good student enactment she, like Leslie, is repeating, just as the school told her to do, rather than innovating.

ABIGAIL: GOOD STUDENTS TEST WELL

Abigail was also a student in Ronald's 7th-grade honors social studies class. Her performance of self was that of a cool, smart, nonchalant student in her dress, her demeanor, and in her daybook. She resisted the narrative of order and control inscribed on her body by the school uniform by wearing it in a snug fit, with her plain, light blue shirt unbuttoned at the top, revealing a white spaghetti-strapped camisole underneath and just a hint of cleavage. Her hair always seemed to be in the process of a new style. She would constantly work on it in class, often walking out into the hall with half of it styled and the other half sticking straight up. She described her activities outside of school as doing her homework, texting her friends, and wrapping her hair. In her dress, mannerisms, and textual performance, Abigail embodies the at-risk student as described in the urban school reform narrative. However, negotiations of the various narratives of her life outside of school and those of the school construct a discourse identity of a good at-risk student in the context of Rosa Parks Middle School and earn her a place in honors classes. Her overall GPA is a high C with her best grades being in the tested areas of math and English. She was in all honors classes because of high scores on the state standardized reading and math tests.

In the new social situation of a group interview with me, she improvised good student by answering every question I asked first of the four girls and with detail as emphasized by the school and Achieve3000. Her performance of self was enthusiastic, bright, and articulate in the interview. However, her daybook was nearly empty, and in class, she chatted constantly with other students rather than paying attention to Ronald. She was so convincing in her role in the interview, that even though I had seen her in Ronald's class numerous times and had combed through her daybook, I thought I had her confused with another student until I went back through her writing samples after the interview. In the interview, she, like Leslie and Erin, found a way to perform good student, by giving back the information she'd been given.

As I mentioned, there was very little in Abigail's daybook. She started a sentence in response to a prompt and then never finished, as if she'd been interrupted in some way. And yet, she was more than happy to share it with me, even digging it out of the stack in the back of the room for me so that she'd be sure I had it. Her test score on the same West African slave trade unit that Leslie mentioned studying for was 58%, and yet in the interview, she talked about the test and studying for it with easy confidence. In class, she talked quietly with other students, laughing and giggling, but also raised her hand to answer questions.

Abigail had not been in Samuel's class where the students wrote the Holocaust diaries, but she had heard about it. She made a bid to be recognized as good student by answering my question about writing in Ronald's class by referring to the diary writing they have done for him. Abigail negotiated the dominant testing and accountability narrative of writing in the school along with what she knew about the narrative I had brought as one of the writing consultants. She said, "Well, we were writing the diary entries acting like we were African and it makes us feel like we were actually there and we get to experience how they felt when they were on the ship." In her description of the assignment, Abigail ventriloquated the reason both Samuel and Ronald gave me for diary writing, explaining to me that it was important for the students to experience what life was like in order to make history more real. For her, in social studies the point was for she and her classmates (we) to "feel" like other people, by taking on another identity.

Abigail took on an agentive role by identifying herself as a member of Ronald's class engaged in the practice of diary writing by saying " . . . we were writing diary entries." She made this class membership significant by saying *we* rather than *I*. She claimed power for herself and her classmates, saying that "we were writing" rather than *we were told to,* or *he said to.* From this agentive stance, she constructed a relationship between the activity of writing and "acting like we were Africans." Her use of the words "acting like" constructed the activity as taking on a pretend identity, rather than composing of self that would connect the "Africans" to the experience of the students in the class, which was my purpose as well as Ronald's for the assignment. Her words "and it makes us feel like we were there" constructed these actions of writing and acting as having the power to "makes us feel." She continued to say "and we get to experience how they felt," valuing the feelings the activity evokes when she said "we *get* to experience." Her use of the word *get*, rather than *have to* or *supposed to* signified that she saw this experience as valuable and worthwhile for "us" feeling like "they felt." Like Leslie and Erin, Abigail is improvising a performance of giving back the information given to her. Abigail does this from an agentive stance, bidding to be recognized as active rather than passive, in her performance of good student.

However, of the three diary entries that were assigned to the class, the following is all that Abigail turned in.

> Hello my name is Thamble gunnogie I am african.
>
> The day I was captured they came and put shakles on my hands and chains on my feet.
>
> On the slave trip it was horrible, discuting. The

Like the other sparse entries in Abigail's daybook, this one seemed unfinished. She began to give back the information she had learned in class about slave ships, but then she did not complete the assignment. She described shackles and chains as well as disgusting conditions, but she stopped mid-sentence at "The." So while she constructed this writing as important and valuable in her interview, she did not complete it. In her negotiation of the various narratives of writing at Rosa Parks Middle School and her experience in school, her "doing" of the work is enough for her to "feel" in a position to claim good student. It is enough doing to see herself in this way and speak to me with authority. From her agentive positionality she saw her writing as signaling her understanding of what "we" are learning and experiencing in social studies.

Abigail explains a little later in the interview how her writing in English class differs from her writing in social studies class:

> Well, writing in English class, we're doing like essays and then we come in here and we do diary entries, so it's like we do poetry writing, essay writing in [Mr. T's]

class, and then we come to [Ronald's] class and we do diary entries and stuff, so it's real different.

The structure of Abigail's answer mimicked the formula for a compare and contrast essay that Tallulah and I observed the students and teachers using in many Rosa Parks Middle School classrooms in preparation for the state writing assessments. There is a topic sentence, "Well writing in English class . . . ." Then a clear contrast was set up with the words "we're doing like essays and then we come in here and do diary entries." She then set up examples of the contrast saying "so it's like we do poetry writing, essay writing in [Mr. T's] class, and then we come to [Ronald's] class and we do diary entries and stuff." Finally, she ended with a concluding thought when she says "so it's real different."

This may be a performance of the essay style, or it may be her thinking process. She performed good student by calling on what she's been taught about answering school essay questions. Her answer set up a difference between writing in social studies and writing in English. In both classes writing is commodified as a thing "we do," rather than a process. And "doing" this writing is something that makes her a good student. However, the doing in English and social studies is "real different."

When Abigail said "we're doing like essays, and then we come in here and we do diary entries, so it's like we do poetry writing, essay writing in [Mr. T's] class," she constructed school writing as something she and her classmates "do," saying "we" are "doing" essays, and poetry and "we do diary entries" rather than we write them. Abigail is negotiating the different narratives of writing in the school: the testing and accountability urban reform narrative like that of Achieve3000 and the Writing Project narrative that I've brought, along with narratives of how to be a good student in order to perform good student for me in this moment. In both narratives, writing is a commodified thing that the students "do." And the "doing" marks them as good students in the honors classes. "Stuff" in Ronald's class differs for the performance of self in English, where the good student there doesn't "feel" in the same way. In English class she completed her assignments, where in social studies, she only had to "feel" just a small written bit to "get" the feeling of what it was like on the ship. The rigors of essay writing and poetry, to Abigail, are more what school is really about—the expected (not the different). In social studies (with these diaries) feeling is crucial, and the dominant socializing discourses of the school attempt to help students sort out which feelings are appropriate—feelings that are covered up in the school uniforms that are supposed to make the students feel and look alike.

For Abigail, as for Leslie and Erin, writing is a commodified thing in her negotiations of the various narratives in Rosa Parks Middle School. The writing Abigail is doing in English class is more recognizable to her as school writing and therefore the thing that is important to her "good student" performance of self. However, she recognizes being interviewed by a university consultant as something good students do, and so she improvised that social situation based on her experience of how to enact good student, responding in essay fashion, and giving back what the teachers say. While Abigail's good student discourse identity is constructed of an agentive stance and resistance to the institutional identity inscribed on her body through the school uniform and doing work without question, her giving-back bid for good student in her talk about her writing is still socializing into the "at-risk" institutional identity and is potentially reproductive.

REPRODUCING GOOD "AT-RISK" STUDENT

Leslie, Erin, and Abigail all enact good student discourse identities as they improvise the activity of writing in new situations and participate in the new social situation of being interviewed by a university researcher. Each constructs writing as a commodified thing that brings students success in the figured world of Rosa Parks Middle School. They draw on the various narratives of writing and performing student in the world of Rosa Parks Middle School, and their negotiations of those narratives result in different performances of good student. Leslie is the most recognizable good student who does every assignment in exactly the way her teachers instruct. Her success in doing so allows her to construct the identity of successful student who will be able to go to college and be a successful adult. Erin has found one area that allows her to construct herself as a successful writer and thus student, and she goes out of her way to continue replicating that experience, even outside of school. However, she does not carry the ability to give back what the teacher is saying across subject areas in the way Leslie does. Abigail identified the writing activity that matters in the construction of her good student identity, and she chose to spend her time on that activity and let other, less important writing assignments slide.

Though the performances are different, each girl is reproducing the socialization process of school without question. Each of them negotiates the various narratives of the school and understands the role of good student as giving back on various levels, and the at-risk institutional identity that urban school reform inscribes on each of the girls. These three students do not question the value of doing certain kinds of writing, or of performing good student, for me, the university researcher. Even Abigail, who isn't actually completing the daybook writing or studying for social studies talks like a good social studies student for me rather than openly questioning the assignments that she has chosen not to do. When she describes her English class writing, the writing she does value, she calls on that valuable essay form in order to continue her good student improvisation. Each of these students, their writing, and their talk about writing, illustrate how schooling in the United States is socializing students and is potentially reproductive. They show how the cycle of social positioning is continued by the socialization process of schooling.

In the next chapter, I will examine the writing and the talk about writing of a resistant student as she negotiates various narratives in Rosa Parks Middle School to do her homework. This student's negotiations are discordant with the recognized narratives of the school and in that opens a space for potential change.

6:

BEING "BAD"

MAKING CRITIQUE VISIBLE

Jada was a 6th grader in Samuel's social studies class. Her teachers described her as having an attitude problem and being a student they were very concerned about. This was Jada's performance of in-school self, who she was in the narrative of Rosa Parks Middle School. Jada's uniform fit but was not snug or revealing. She wore the plain blue shirt and khaki pants, and her hair was always swept back into a simple ponytail at the base of her neck. Bits and pieces escaped from the hair bow and stuck out around her head. The order and control of the uniform was inscribed on her body, but she resisted any attempts to make it look anything other than imposed on her. It did not fit her performance of self, but she did not make any attempt to make this lack of fit any less obvious. On the day that the students emotionally shared their Holocaust diaries in Samuel's class, Jada didn't cry with the others. She sat in the corner, doodling on her paper, appearing stoic. She seemed walled off from the rest of the class, keeping her eyes on her own paper, but with head held high in open disapproval of what was happening in the room, performing her "resistant student" discourse identity.

Jada's performance is markedly different from the students in Chapter 5. They all had experience performing the discourse identity of good student. Being tracked into the honors social studies class in 7th grade marks success in their performances. Their success potentially reproduces their class position because their institutional identity is at-risk student, and therefore the good student in the figured world of Rosa Parks Middle School is also an at-risk student. This institutional identity controls what is recognized as good student in that figured world, recycling what the teacher or a text has said and not deviating from that narrative in any way. Creativity and innovation are not valued for the good at-risk student in the same way it is valued for good students in the successful school down the road.

In this chapter, I examine Jada's language and performance as a resistant student identity. Like the other students in this study, the institution of school has inscribed an at-risk institutional identity onto her. In the moment of the Holocaust diary assignment, she improvised a performance of good student by writing a diary entry, and talking to the consultants about her work. Her improvisation, however, was discordant with the at-risk institutional identity because she did not repeat back the information given to her. In fact, without knowing it, Jada made a bid for good student with an innovative response that would be recognized in a "successful" school because Jada's improvisation of good student temporarily opened up space for social change. Rather than simply repeating information like a good at-risk student, she questions and innovates. The material result of Jada's improvisation, however, was not change. In fact, because of her resistance to the socialization of schooling in which good students give back what they have been given, both on this assignment and in others, she was marked as bad and problematic by the institution of school, and she doesn't get to go to the honors class in 7th grade. As an at-risk student, she doesn't have the social power to be innovative. On the surface, Jada's performance of resistance makes her appear to be just another troubled student. However, her resistance makes the socialization process of school visible when we take the time to dig below the surface to look at the world her language is constructing.

In this chapter I look closely at both Jada's Holocaust diary entry and her own take on it in order to explore her negotiations of the various narratives present in the school and in her life as she attempts to fulfill the assignment. Her improvisation disrupts the socializing narrative of schooling in subtle ways that are still recognizable in the world of the school, and this disruption holds transformative potential for the reproductive model of schooling in the more successful good student performances in Chapter 5.

JADA: RESISTING THROUGH INNOVATION

I was interested in Jada's piece because she was one of only two students in the class who chose to write about liberation from the concentration camps, a narrative of hope, and yet one that didn't conform to the parameters of acceptable writing in this instance. When the academic facilitator and Samuel excitedly showed me the student work, they did not show me Jada's entry. Later, as we talked about what to do with the work, they mentioned that some students wrote about the Americans fighting, which they considered to be "too violent" because of the use of guns depicted in the narratives. The other pieces of writing, much like Erin's, focused on horrific and hopeless moments of capture and starvation with descriptions of the death of loved ones in gas chambers and the crematorium, emulating the diary entries in the film that they had watched in class. Yet these other entries were not described as violent. Jada's draft did not proceed from a victim's persona; rather, Jada implicated the Holocaust victims in an iconic American narrative of pride in staying strong until the American rescuers arrived. Jada's piece did not evoke the violence of the battle scenes as described in some of the other diary entries, yet it did offer a counter to the idea of Holocaust diary as it is represented in the work of the other students and in the film they watched. This counter idea marked her piece for both Samuel and the academic facilitator as "not worth my time" because she had not "gotten" the film. Below is Jada's entry:

April 12 1945

I was just sitting there when I saw a beautiful sight over the hills. I was so happy that my people was saved. It was still painful to know that my family was still gone. To know that people was still suffering. Although people was still dieing. Then when they came to get me I couldn't move. I tryed to smile but my face was numb from laying on the hard cold ground. I saw the other people crying and smiling. I saw the soilders picking up kids and kissing them. It was painful to know while the resucing was happening people were still dieing. While I was there I saw people trying to stand and smile. Me and my dad were the only ones still their in my family. I felt like I was on steel. It was cold. I was so happy that people was able to stay strong and live until the United States got there. It was just a beautiful scene. Later on that day people was getting put in schools. They were having a good time but they will always remember the day they was torchered.

While certainly not a happy piece of writing, Jada's focus on liberation is markedly distinct from Erin's entry and those of the rest of the class in that she paints scenes of hope. She mentions a "beautiful sight" in the first line, and the idea of being saved in the second sentence. She then evoked of scene of people, including herself, trying to smile through the pain that they have endured and the difficulty of the mixed feelings she had being rescued and knowing others were still suffering. Here she showed understanding of the complex feelings of being rescued, and the difficulties of the concentration camps. Then she evoked the American narrative of pride and heroism when she wrote, "I was so happy that people was able to stay strong and live until the United States got there. It was just a beautiful scene." Her focus was on the joy of liberation and the idea of new beginnings. The narrative Jada evoked was very patriotic, reminiscent of U.S. war movies while showing understanding of the hardships faced by the people in the concentration camps and ending with a scene of hope and the belief in the narrative of the power of education by mentioning that people were sent to schools.

Though the there are errors in the writing, she shows a rather sophisticated understanding of what it would have been like to be rescued from a concentration camp through her understanding of the emotional complexity such an experience would involve. However, this sophistication goes unremarked upon by her teacher and the academic facilitator because it is not what was in the film; she went beyond that narrative, and that does not fit the institutional identity of an at-risk student. Her answer is considered wrong.

I interviewed Jada because I was interested in why she chose to write about the liberation. Jada's enactment of good student identity is complicated. She brought a recognizable American-hero narrative in order to resist the expected Holocaust victim-atrocity narrative. She did the assignment (something she rarely did), but she did so by nominating the Americans-to-the-rescue story, one that would be acceptable in some instances but not in *this* instance because it did not recycle the narrative of the film. In her bid for good student as she negotiated with the dominant narratives, she deviated from the script of recycling information, resisted the at-risk institutional identity, and made a bid for good student that would be recognized in an upper-middle-class school where students are expected to create and innovate even if they also repeat an idealized view of American hero myths.

TRYING ON THE AMERICAN DREAM

Tallulah asked Jada to read her diary entry while being videotaped, and then tell us about why she wrote it, and how she felt about what she wrote. She was aware that she was being videotaped and that we would use the footage to publish the work of the class. As she participated in the process, she continued to negotiate the various narratives of the school world and her role there, as well as her bid for good student (even though her bid failed because the authority figures at Rosa Parks Middle School saw it as resistant). She dutifully answered the questions set before her, claiming her own power, but distancing herself from the activity of doing the school assignment by performing her resistant student self. But in response to Tallulah's follow-up question about schoolwork she shifted away from her own power and ideas and ventriloquated the "American Dream" narrative of urban school reform and the illustrations on the posters around the school, improvising a way to enact cooperative student. Jada's interview with Tallulah follows:

J: Okay, I felt like writing this because it was just history and schoolwork and um, and I felt sad because, it was people were dying and stuff and they had to wait for the United States and the rest of the countries to get there and get help. And I felt like sharing this in school because it was, oh, like me, I'm just like cool and stuff, so I just wanted to share it, just so that they would know I could write it write the diary entries and stuff.

T: So that your classmates would know? Yeah, so, tell me a little bit more about what you said at the start about it being schoolwork.

J: Oh Yeah. It's like, it's like that you should always do your schoolwork and uh always uh, uh, . . . just to do your schoolwork, so that you can get a grade and, and a higher grade so that you will be able to do good in school so that you can go to college. (Jada's interviews are broken down into stanzas in the Appendix.)

The beginning of the interview represents Jada's on-camera answers to our questions: Why did you write this, how did you feel about the writing, and why did you share it? A closer look will reveal the world Jada was constructing as she answered the questions and responded to the follow-up question.

Jada began by saying, "Okay," signifying that she was going to cooperate by answering the questions Tallulah asked her, and she then claimed her own power in this cooperation, while taking an agentive stance using *I* statements in answer to Tallulah's questions. Her language constructed her as having the power to choose to do her schoolwork (or not) when she said "I felt like writing this" and "I felt like sharing this," rather than *I was supposed to,* or *I had to,* signaling that though the writing of the diary and then the sharing of it was something asked of her by her teacher, she participated because she "*felt* like" writing and sharing. At the same time, she distanced herself from the activity of doing the writing (schoolwork) by saying "it was *just* history and schoolwork," constructing "history" and "schoolwork" as not very valuable to her with the word *just*. She also distanced herself from the activity of sharing in the classroom with her use of the word *just* when she said, "so I just wanted to share it just so that they would know I could write it." She claimed further authority with the words "I felt like . . . ." Her assertions built the identity and her performance of self as resistant student, of someone who would not have done what her teacher asked her to do if she did not feel like doing it. This resistant identity marks her as different from the good at-risk students who do as they are told simply because they were told to. Jada instead thinks about whether she feels like doing what is asked of her, enacting a more critical stance.

Then, halfway through the sentence, there was a switch in the way Jada constructed her feelings. Before, she was saying that she did the schoolwork because "she just felt like it," but here she engaged with Tallulah about what was happening in class the day everyone was reading. She said, "um, and I felt sad because, it was people were dying and stuff . . ." She constructed her feelings about the Holocaust as sad, making a bid for her feelings as correct as linked with the crying the other students were doing. She also builds a relationship between this "sad" feeling and people dying. When she added "and stuff," she signified that there is more to the story that caused her sadness; however, she chose not to share that information with Tallulah. She went on to say that she was sad because "they had to wait for the United States and the rest of the countries to get there and get help." Here she built a relationship between her sad feelings and the fact that it was sad that people had to wait to be saved, signifying that waiting to be saved is a sad thing to her. She also constructed the victims of the Holocaust as waiting for someone else to save them and unable to help themselves and her feelings about that as sad.

In this same sentence, Jada also evokes a patriotic narrative that echoes the narrative seen on the posters in the hallways as she constructs the United States as the leader in the help operation, choosing to name only the United States, placing it first and referring to "the rest of the countries." She chose to nominate the American patriotic narrative to negotiate her cooperation in the activity of writing about and talking about the Holocaust in order to be recognized for doing something that a good student would do. She did not choose to recycle the narrative of the film, evoking a resistant student discourse identity, but she did choose a narrative that was recognizable in the world of Rosa Parks Middle School.

By saying that she chose to share her writing in school "because [she] felt like it," Jada continued to build her identity as resistant student with the power to choose whether she does what is asked of her in school. She distanced herself from this sharing activity by saying "I'm *just* like cool and stuff." She constructed her power and distance as "cool," but "and stuff" signified that there is more to this story that she chose not to share with Tallulah or on camera. Her language built a distanced relationship with the people in the room with the words "*just* so they would know." She also signified that there is more that she wants them to know she can do beside write the diaries by adding "and stuff" to the sentence "I could write it, write diaries and stuff." Her language builds a relationship between her choice to cooperate here, when she is usually resistant, and others' knowing her abilities and recognizing her as a good student.

When Tallulah pointed back to Jada's mention of "schoolwork" by saying "So, tell me a little bit more about what you said at the start about it being schoolwork," it signaled to Jada that Tallulah was really only interested in schoolwork, and therefore was not interested in what Jada has said about sadness, sharing her writing, or the Holocaust. Jada signaled that she understood that she had been wrong so far and that she now knew what Tallulah wanted from her by saying "Oh yeah." In her improvisation to cooperate, Jada drew on her understanding of what is acceptable in the figured world of Rosa Parks Middle School. She ventriloquated the recognizable American Dream narrative of working hard and pulling oneself up by the bootstraps (another narrative played out on the walls of the school). She signaled that this is what she understood was required of her in this activity when she said "It's like, it's like that you should always do your schoolwork and uh always uh, uh, . . . just to do your schoolwork, so that you can get a grade and, and a higher grade so that you will be able to do good in school so that you can go to college."

However, in this move to cooperate, Jada switched to *you* statements, signaling that this is something other people should do and constructing herself as distanced from this activity, maintaining her resistant performance of self. She further distances herself with the phrase "*just* do your schoolwork" and signals that getting it done is all there is to schoolwork. The *so* statements ("so you can get a grade," "so that you will be able to do good in school," "so that you can go to college") signified a progression, connecting doing schoolwork to getting to college. In this section of the interview, Jada constructed a world where schoolwork is about getting a grade and getting to college. By switching to *you* statements, she constructed her own identity as distanced from a person who would "just" do these things without question and performed her resistant self even as she cooperated.

Jada was not comfortable performing good student in the way she thought Tallulah wanted her too. Her distancing language can be understood as what Bettie (2003) calls "attempting to pass." Because of her institutional identity of at-risk student, and the narrative of her lived history that will not allow her to simply recycle information like the other good students in the school, she improvises an innovative answer. But she doesn't feel comfortable with it, as if she doesn't belong.

TAKING A QUIZ

I interviewed Jada again later because I was interested in why she chose to write about the moment of liberation. Below is a snippet from my interview with her. Here, Jada was negotiating her role as good student at Rosa Parks Middle School with the outside university researcher. In this interview, I was trying to understand Jada's views of her writing and building rapport with Jada. In the section of our conversation I've selected below, there is a shift in Jada's view of me as I filled in what I expected Jada to say and constructed what evoked a quiz question for her.

C: Can you tell me a little bit about why you choose to write about this part of the concentration camp in your piece?

J: Oh I chose this one because I didn't want to cry in front of all them girls so I just wrote about the end and like the part where they came and saved everybody.

C: That makes sense. It makes a lot of sense. So you liked this happier part; it seemed a little safer to write about; I understand that! You did a really great job with it. How do you feel about that piece of writing?

J: I feel good because it was sad. Everybody was crying and stuff and uh, and I felt like writing this uh, uh, hmmmm. . . . I don't know why I felt like writing this. I just felt like writing something. I didn't want to do my homework.

C: Was this homework?

J: [nods]

Jada began with the word "Oh," rather than *well* or simply *I did this because,* in a dismissive, this-is-easy tone of voice. She claimed her power throughout by using *I* statements, placing herself in complete control of her actions. She let me know that crying "in front of all them girls" was not an acceptable activity to her. She did not say that crying, or even crying in front of people, is a problem for her. For her, the issue lay in crying in front of all of the girls in her class. Her language built a relationship with the girls of the class in which crying is not acceptable. It also built a distance between her and the interviewer. Jada's language constructed a disconnect between the activity of the classroom in that moment and her own rules and understanding of how to be in the world, and the world of the school. Her language also constructed an identity for herself as confident in her way of negotiating that disconnect.

When she said "so I just wrote about the end," the words *so* and *just* distanced her from this unacceptable (to her) activity of crying, and she built an identity for herself of having ease with the way she has negotiated this disconnect. She improvised by ventriloquating the recognizable American patriotic narrative. She claimed her power to choose a different narrative from the film when she said "*I liked* the part at the end." She didn't like the part portrayed in the film, and so she chose not to write about it, not to repeat what the film and her teacher gave her.

As a novice interviewer, I made several grievous errors in my response that signified to Jada that I thought her answer was wrong and signaled to her that we were engaged in a right-and-wrong-answer activity, like a school quiz. My double assertion "That makes sense, it makes a lot of sense" signaled that she could have answered in a way that did not make sense. Then I revised her answer for her by telling her what she really meant, saying "You liked this happier part." My language then solidified our relationship as person who knows (me) and person who does not know (Jada) by asserting that she chose this part because "it seemed safer to write about." I asserted that my answer was right by saying "I can understand that." By using "I" here, I claimed the power of deciding what is correct and understandable and then built my position as person with the power to judge by saying "You did a good job with it." Further, I did not explain what exactly she had done a good job with. "It" could be writing, talking to me, or choosing a topic. By not specifying, I signaled that "it" really is not that important as long as I said that it is good. My language constructed Jada as someone who does not need to think about those sorts of details because I was the one with the power to do that. It also signified that her improvisation was incorrect because I revised it for her and explained that my revision was understandable.

My response constructed Jada as student and emphasized that we were involved in a school activity, invoking the narrative in which the adult asks questions that she already knows the answer to and the student tries to get them right. My revision of her response and my vague comment about her doing a good job indirectly suggested that I am not really interested in her actual thoughts and ideas, or her innovations. Jada perceived that my next question "How do you feel about that piece of writing?" was not a real question, in that I was not interested in her answer, but rather in the correct answer that I already had in mind and that she must find if she wanted to be identified as a good student in our relationship.

After my response, there was a shift in Jada's language that showed that she had understood my indirect speech act and that she was actually answering quiz questions instead of having a conversation. She began to enact good student, answering the question. She claimed her comfort with her choice, saying "I feel good" and then paused after "because" before saying "it was sad." "It was sad" builds a connection with her feelings and those of the rest of the class, constructing her as good because she felt "sad" like the others—she felt the right way. She mirrors my vague language by not explaining whether "it" is the information she had learned about the Holocaust; her writing; or her classmates' and teachers' reactions to the information, the writing, or the reading. She began the next statement by explaining that "Everybody was crying and stuff." She did not use *we,* and so maintained her distance from the activity of crying. "And stuff" indicates that there were other things happening that she was distancing herself from as well. The distancing allowed her to continue her resistant student performance of self while trying to be good student by ventriloquating that crying narrative of the classroom.

She made one more attempt to answer the quiz question, beginning with the question stem, "I felt like writing this . . ." She enacted thinking about the answer with "hmmmm" and then dropped the good student identity with the answer "I don't know . . ." Here, Jada's language quickly reclaimed her authority and challenged the construction of herself as wrong because she does not know the answer. She said "I just felt like writing something." Her language here reclaimed the agentive stance as she asserted that she did the writing because *she* felt like it, not because she was told to and complied. She then positioned herself further away from the compliant student role by explaining that she did not want to do her homework. Her language built a challenge to my authority as the researcher who was telling her what she meant and why she chose to write what she did. When I asserted "So you liked this happier part; It seemed a little safer to write about," my language constructed the identity of her need for "safety," and it did not fit with her way of knowing and being and the identity that she enacted at the beginning. She rejected my revision of her answer and her identity after trying on good student, and she re-asserts herself as having a resistant discourse identity. My assertion that this *was* indeed homework, through the question "Was this homework?", ended the interview. She did nod, slightly, in response, but she was no longer willing to talk to me because I had claimed my role as one who is to show her how her answers are wrong. She, however, is not interested in that construction of her ideas.

MOMENTS OF POSSIBILITY

Jada's activities of writing about a hopeful moment at the end of the Holocaust, refusing to cry with and in front of her classmates, and yet rejecting the self-identification as someone in need of safety are all significant. They illustrate counter-activities and counter-outcomes to the dominant insistence on compliance and standardization. Jada tempers her resistance carefully, moving right along the boundaries of what she knows to be acceptable in school, nominating other narratives that are present in the school though not in the film. Jada is negotiating what she knows of the way to be in school with what she knows about the way to be in the world. She has done the writing her teacher assigned and nominates the American patriotic narrative—one that is recognizable in the figured world of Rosa Parks Middle School despite its contrast to the dominant narrative given in the assignment and class. She has cooperated by allowing herself to be interviewed and recorded reading the piece and agreeing to be a part of a study with a researcher. When, in two different settings, she interprets cues from Tallulah and me that she is not really answering in an appropriate way, she dutifully modifies her answers, moving away from her ideas to what she believes to be correct in her narrative of doing school. She is not willing to comply with the crying in which the other students and teachers engage, nor is she willing to perform by answering a question that she feels constructs her as needing safety.

When I revised her answers in conversation and when Tallulah pointed out the inconsistencies in Jada's own language about her notion of schoolwork, it served to remind Jada that her ways of being and knowing do not fit in this instance of the socializing institution of schooling in the United States. She has been falsely passing. She doesn't belong in this good student role. In both cases, she attempts to enact the good at-risk student identity that we want from her, as indicated through our acts of language. On camera, she succeeds in narrating the American Dream narrative about schoolwork, though she carefully removes herself from it. However, with me, she attempted to answer in the way she believes I'm asking her to, but in the end she refused when I continued to position her as wrong. She chose silence, staying recognizable within the world of good at-risk student by not contradicting me, but she refused to engage in the non-conversation any longer and maintained her resistant performance of self.

Jada's improvisations in her constructions of self in the school world are moments of possibility, and she represents the ways in which students and teachers possess "a modicum of agency" (Holland, et al., 1998) within the socially constructed figured world of school. Therefore, she is not doomed to simply reproduce the dominant and dominating narratives and be reproduced by them. Jada gives us an image of possibility, even though the material result for Jada in this moment is still to be marked as resistant. Students and teachers working collectively, noticing the socializing narratives at work and actively listening to each other, can work in solidarity to resist the repetitive give-back-the-right-answer socialization that constructs being a good at-risk student. As the resistant student, Jada foregrounds our notions (mine, Tallulah's, her teachers', Rosa Parks Middle School's, and the institution of schooling's) of acceptability and makes the socialization process very visible to us if we care to look. Her moments of resistance are mini-critiques of the dominant and dominating narratives. Jada represents possibility in that she has shown, through her writing, that the at-risk institutional identity that insists on students giving back is not fixed or static, or even "True."

7:

CONCLUSION

A CALL FOR CRITIQUE OF THE TESTING AND ACCOUNTABILITY NARRATIVE OF SCHOOLING

How does the story of students and teachers working with writing in social studies at Rosa Parks Middle School reflect broader debates about urban schools, school reform, and standardized curricula and testing? The stories of Samuel, Ronald, Erin, Leslie, Abigail, and Jada illustrate the many competing and conflicting narratives students and teachers must negotiate in order to teach writing or to write in an urban middle school. These narrative negotiations illustrate the complexity of writing and teaching writing in this context. Among all the narratives being negotiated, the current urban reform narratives of testing and accountability hold the most power and lead to narrow practices of teaching and learning, particularly in writing instruction, that have students repeating back what they have been told rather than thinking critically and creatively. This repeating back solidifies the students' social position, making the urban reform narrative, particularly that of testing and accountability, complicit in potential social reproduction. However, this is not a hopeless situation. At the same time, other ideas of teaching writing, such as those from the NWP are circulating in schools along with the students' own ideas of how to think, write and be in the world. There is hope in the resistance to the power narrative enacted by these competing narratives. We can see this hope in the stories of Ronald and Jada if we view that resistance as a critique on the system that is serving to keep marginalized students on the margins.

What was our impact on Rosa Parks Middle School? We connected personally with many teachers, but the Writing Project is no longer in the building. We hear from the teachers we worked with and see them in other schools, but they are no longer at Rosa Parks Middle School. Samuel was reassigned to a leadership position at another middle school and from there went on to become an assistant principal in a large high school in the district. Ronald left to work at a charter school where he felt like he would be listened to and where he feels like he has the "freedom to teach," and then he eventually moved to another state do to the same. The first principal, the one we connected with, is gone. The academic facilitator who shot me the excited email is gone. This level of turnover in staff is typical of low-performing schools serving a high-minority population in the district.

Leslie left the school to attend a magnet program. Erin and Abigail finished middle school and moved on, but they entered high school behind other honors 8th graders because Rosa Parks Middle School did not offer an algebra course like middle schools in the district serving upper-middle-class students. Jada left the school at the end of her 6th grade year, moving out of the community completely. The school still ranks as low-performing according to state and federal tests. As a "turn around" school, Rosa Parks Middle School is turning in yet another direction while test scores remain low, the teachers and staff stay overworked and overwhelmed, and the students stay in places of poverty and marginalization.

We were not invited back to Rosa Parks Middle School after the grant cycle that funded our work ended. Our emails and phone calls were not returned by the administration. The partnership with Rosa Parks Middle School has dissolved, and we have wondered what we actually did there. What we've come to know in all of our many conversations and what we've learned from Samuel, Ronald, Jada, Leslie, Erin, Abigail, and all the other students is that while struggle is an important part of change we were all struggling with the wrong things. As writing consultants, instead of stopping to see the various narratives we were working within and against and attempting to understand how power was at work within those narratives so that we might critique dominant narratives for the benefit of our students, we and the teachers and administrators were struggling against one another.

That said, answering the question of how could we have done a better job is complicated. The issue is a systemic one. In many ways the answer to the question is the writing of this book, illuminating the ways in which the power narratives of urban school reform and testing and accountability were taking over that of the National Writing Project in our work. The NWP narrative sees the importance of teachers developing deep, trusting relationships with each other so that they might think and work together. However, the power narratives see teachers as transient, which made this nearly impossible, especially at Rosa Parks Middle School where the principal was replaced and teachers were removed due to strategic staffing or left due to the poor working conditions. The school was also populated by Teach for America teachers, educators who by nature of the program are only expected to be in the school and the profession for a few years. The NWP narrative also views teachers as professionals who work together to meet the needs of individual students. The scripted lessons and programs like Achieve3000 view teachers as little more than automatons. NWP views students as thinkers and writers who can connect their lives to the curriculum. The power narrative views them as people who need to recycle the information given to them without question. The narratives were clearly at odds and the power narratives had, well, the power. Here, I will outline how the power narratives take over what well-meaning people (all of the teachers, administrators, and consultants involved) are attempting to accomplish and offer strategies for opening up conversations about these competing narratives as a way to work toward this much-needed systemic change. I will end with some images of hope.

CLASHING NARRATIVES AND POWER: A RECAP

The students, teachers, principals, and consultants were all working hard at Rosa Parks Middle School trying to produce talented, engaged students, but the various narratives constructing the school competed with each other while the children were constructing their own identities and knowledge (as we all are) within and against dominant narratives. The power narratives of education written on and through the children's bodies did not produce critically engaged democratic citizens as promised; at best, they produced identities who did as they were told, and whose competing identities were busting out of the seams.

At Rosa Parks Middle School, when the students sat down to write in social studies class, they were negotiating the testing and accountability narrative of literacy that defined writing as a set of skills and rules to be mastered that necessitates a standard, uniform, and measurable form. This narrative positioned them as at-risk students who were only capable of writing highly structured essays that repeat information given to them as if they were filling out worksheets. In contrast, they were also negotiating competing narratives of literacy brought by outside writing consultants, which call the testing and accountability narrative into question. The Writing Project narrative viewed writing as situated within particular contexts (conversations, histories, discourses) and as a way of thinking and connecting new information with known information. Further, it viewed the testing and accountability narrative as limited and limiting and used writing to inquire into such legitimizing power structures.

The students were also negotiating various narratives from the other figured worlds in their lives as they responded to the ways these institutional narratives positioned them. Leslie responded by doing as she is told. Erin responded by repeating one moment where she felt successful. Abigail responded through dress, accessorizing her uniform in a way that did not comply with the middle management expectation, and by testing well, completing work only in the tested classes where she felt it important. Jada responded with resistance to the power narrative and the way it positioned her on a daily basis.

As students negotiated these narratives, they encountered new social situations and improvised in order to enact student. Abigail had to improvise to figure out what to do when writing is about feeling rather than repeating narratives she had been taught in class. Jada found herself wanting to respond to what she was learning about the Holocaust and decided to do her homework as well to as cooperate with the consultants when they wanted to interview her. She had to improvise how to be a person who does her homework and cooperated in a way that made sense in what she knew about the narratives of the school, the consultants, and her narratives of how to be a person in the world.

The complexity of student identity formation was not apparent in the long columns of standardized test score data that named the students, and thereby the teachers, the administrators, and the school as in need of intervention. However, the scores had the power to define the types of intervention the students received. At Rosa Parks Middle School, those interventions included the Achieve3000 computer program that tells students what to copy from an article and paste into blanks. Achieve3000, its corporate body, and the school administration called that writing. The school administration also specified a policy that focused on preparation for multiple-choice tests rather than writing in order to focus on raising scores. In the end, these interventions did not work, yet the interventions were not considered the problem. The students, then, were the ones deemed incapable of success because after all of this help and opportunity, they still could not read at a basic level or write without grammatical errors. The test scores had the power to reproduce society as it was, securely fastening the students into their places of poverty and marginalization, and then to blame the students and their teachers for not working hard enough.

AGENCY: ROOM FOR CHANGE

In her book *Women Without Class*, Bettie (2003) describes the power of institutions, such as schools, as well as the agency people have in terms of identity performance and performativity. For Bettie, *performance* implies agency and enables us to think about the exception to the rule, for example, the at-risk kid who performs as successful by "negotiating an inherited and chosen identity" (p. 192). In this book, I talked about this phenomena as discourse identity. Performativity theorizes the "structural, institutionalized inequalities [that] preexist and for the most part produce . . . performances" (p. 192) without the social actors recognizing it, or institutional identity. As the students at Rosa Parks Middle School worked to perform good student, the dominant and dominating narratives that constructed them as at-risk students produced their performances. That social, historical power was ever-present in the socialization happening in the school (including the actions of the writing consultants). Jada took an agentic stance, performing successful student, resisting the give-back-what-you've-been-given narrative of good at-risk student, including when I tried to construct her as needing safety. However, due to the power of the dominating narrative, her performance had the material result of marking her as bad.

Jada's resistance to the at-risk construction and the socialization of the school through the uniform and other narratives of order and control, as well as to the ideas of how to respond to the Holocaust, can also be recognized as a critique of the way the institution positioned her in society. Like the working-class high school students in Bettie's study who were able to see the "structures of exclusion at work" when they were "exposed to middle class cultural forms" in the college-prep classes, Jada's resistance makes the socialization of the school world very visible. The material result of her resistance (further marginalization) demonstrates the necessity for a discourse of critique in classrooms, in schools, and among intervening consultants. Lyotard (1979) argues that consensus is not only less than ideal but "elicits complicity with totalizing regimes of knowledge and truth" where those with the most power get to name "truth" and "knowledge" (p. 45).

Jada, in juxtaposition to the good students, performed identities much like the teachers and administrators who seemed resistant to our ideas and those teachers who were considered good in the Writing Project reform narrative. Those resistant to the Writing Project accepted the dominant and dominating testing and accountability narrative of writing by insisting on the repetitive-socializing, recycle-what-is-given-to-you narrative, which pushed the Writing Project's narrative of thinking out loud on paper to the margins. The critique offered by the resistant teachers was that while what we suggested may sound great, or even ideal, their jobs and the lives of their students were at stake if scores weren't raised. It was easy for us to resist the testing and accountability narrative that dictated narrowly structured, formulaic writing and not take it seriously from our position as white middle-class women with university jobs. The teachers and administrators saw our professional development with writing as constructing classroom practices as wrong and bad rather than as a critique of the testing and accountability structure on a broader scale. We failed to recognize how normalized and legitimizing the power narratives are, and we often struggled against each other rather than listening carefully and deeply to the very real, powerful critiques each group offered. All of the people involved—the consultants, the administrators, and the teachers—missed the opportunity to work together against the dominating narrative that produced and maintained this school as one on the margins.

In Appendix I, I have listed possible prompts for discussion between consultants, administrators, and teachers as they begin their work together in the complex figured world of an urban middle school to find ways to develop discourse identities of success rather than being constructed completely by the institutional identity of failure. Given our experiences at Rosa Parks Middle School, these discussions needed to take place not only at the beginning of our work, but throughout our time together.

STEPS TOWARD CHANGE

While our work at Rosa Parks Middle School may not have impacted the school, it did hugely impact the lives of certain teachers who are continuing to teach and to think together about how to engage children as thinkers within the testing and accountability culture, but in schools where their expertise is noticed and called upon. Ronald, for instance, joined a charter school where his desire to integrate writing and thinking in social studies is now celebrated. Though the school leadership team is under testing and accountability mandates like the team at Rosa Parks Middle School, they allow Ronald to engage his students and work with them as writers. He is also called upon to share his work with his colleagues and with parents of the children in his classroom. The focus in his charter school is "both/and" rather than "either/or"—both challenge and engage the students and prepare them for the challenges of testing. In Rosa Parks Middle School it was either prepare students for the test (never do anything but test prep) or lose your job. Those of us committed to regular public schools (nonprofit schools that ideally serve all students no matter what) might learn about how schools without some of the restrictions placed on state/district-sponsored public schools are able to see past the tests to the teachers and children and the quality of educational life worth continuing. While charter schools have been criticized for abusing this freedom in some cases, there is still much to learn from them.

School leaders who envision ways of engaging teachers and students in meaningful learning, rather than ratcheting down and drilling students weekly for "formative" objective assessments, would help to create the conditions for positive impact on student learning. Objective assessments themselves need only be one part of the school portrait. They might be compared to other products of learning, such as portfolios of writing or products produced in project-based learning. These products might be created through the imaginative engagement of children, which in themselves offer critique of the uniformity, sameness, and repetition of standardized work, products of learning that illustrate that education is about working with human beings and all of the complexity that entails, rather than uniform widgets on the factory line.

As the NWP now competes for federal funding, racing to the top right along with and against all school systems, those of us involved with the Writing Project feel the power of the testing and accountability narrative as the funding requires that the program prove it works through measurable results. Although some policies at the state and federal level continue to push the testing and accountability narrative there is also another narrative of resistance, often heard in conversations among parents and teachers about how reductive and disruptive to learning these pressures are. But the pressures from the testing and accountability agenda are so powerful that the cries for accountability drown out competing voices. Parents have a right to understand what is happening in schools and to make informed choices for their children. Deborah Meir says "all parents [and other community members] need ways to make informed judgments about the professional competence of the school" (as cited in Gallagher, 2011, p. 119). The accountability agenda points to standardized testing as the only way to make this happen. But those documenting the problems of objectivist assessment offer other images of possibility (e.g., Gallagher, 2011; Brannon & Scott, 2013), where assessment is something that happens locally, is instruction-driven, is designed by teachers along with their students in classrooms, and is firmly embedded in the ways of being and knowing of the community the school serves. In this view of assessment, teachers and students would be the generators of assessment rather than the targets of it (Gallagher, 2011).

IMAGES OF HOPE

At times this work seems daunting, almost impossible, but as Jean Anyon (1997) says, "visionaries have long maintained that in order to make fundamental change we have to believe that such changes are possible" (p. 165). She lays out a possibility that shows educators working in solidarity with community organizations offering everything from the creating of Work Projects Administration–type jobs to legal services to housing associations and voter registration. Essentially, she calls for the neighborhood school to be the "nuclei where referrals to these economic, political, and social services are made or where the services themselves are provided" (p. 169). Rather than a castle on the hill as a symbol of how the neighborhood and the people in it are wrong and bad, the school can work for change and become the center of critique of a system that feeds the cycle of poverty. Education alone cannot solve the social problem of poverty; however, schools working with other community groups can be the hub where all groups interested in the welfare of children come together.

Youth Roots, a community youth organization in Oakland, California, is another group offering an image of possibility for sustained critique. Here, minority adolescents come together and spend their free time developing a discourse of critique of the systems that keep them on the margins of society and then use it as "artivists" to spread their message. The group tours the country, attending teacher conferences, speaking to educators in powerful young voices about what they and their peers need. They offer images of teachers and children and community groups working together, giving other ways of being and doing.

Some community groups organized by parents and concerned citizens have protested the testing and accountability agenda and the amount of time testing takes away from actual learning in schools. They are making use of technology and social media (Facebook, Twitter) to get their message out and to point to other organizations around the country offering similar critiques. They engage in activities like demonstrations in front of education buildings, dancing with their children in public protest, and asking school boards to consider alternative ways of creating knowledge and identities in schools.

Professional associations such as NWP and the National Council of Teachers of English, like State Departments of Education and local educational systems, are required to prove themselves with measurable results. As professional networks, they have offered ways to collectively voice concerns and offer alternatives. As engaged citizens and as professionals we can use these avenues to build coalitions of resistance and to make visible the consequences of an overpowering testing establishment.

Jada's critique of the socializing narrative of the school also shows us a need for a discourse of critique in educational research. We need more research that answers Foucault's call to map the micro powers in the world. We need to understand how power/knowledge are working in the lives of children and educators and map how marginalization is happening so that there is an ongoing critique of education. Such work requires qualitative studies where the details and contexts are of the upmost importance. Rather than trying to reach consensus about what is causing the achievement gap and producing products to fix it, educational research needs to remain ever vigilant in the analysis of the inescapable socialization of schooling, even in, as Luke (1992) points out, the most emancipating of classroom practices, and critical of the way of those practices limit access to social resources.

GETTING SCHOOLED ON RESISTANCE: CONCLUSIONS

The current climate of education reform based in the market logic of competition and efficiency makes Jada's story, and those of the other teachers, students, and consultants in this study, of utmost importance when viewed through a constructivist lens. The testing and accountability paradigm that is the common sense of the dominant reform policy works to inscribe some students and schools as low performing and others as high achieving through standardized testing. Putting testing in the hands of expert vendors removes the messy, human process of assessment from the hands of teachers and students and is therefore more efficient. Standardized testing "serves as a lever for score-keeping and competition" as schools try to produce the best "widget-education," in order to compete for students, and for funding (Gallagher, 2011, p. 454). This common sense logic sees the people being educated as consumers of knowledge rather than participants in knowledge-making. And in a market environment of competition, someone *must* be left behind; someone must win, and someone must lose.

However, a focus on the complexity of the narratives students negotiate as they construct their student identities illuminates clearly how power/knowledge determines largely who gets to win and who gets to lose. A focus on mapping how marginalization happens offers images of possibility for change. A discourse of critique, where questioning rather than compliance and efficiency are ideal, is in many ways what happened in the moments when Samuel and Ronald and their students were engaged in writing and saw themselves as writers whose words had powerful effects on others. It is crucial to make that critique the norm in our institutions of education, to re-vision "resistant" as "brilliant, engaged student and citizen."

ABOUT THE AUTHOR

Cynthia D. Urbanski, PhD, has worked with writing and writers in some capacity for 30 years. She is the author of *Using the Workshop Approach in the High School English Classroom* (2006, Corwin Press) and co-author of *Thinking Out Loud on Paper* (2008, Heinemann Books) and *Making Middle School* (2020, NCTE). Currently, her projects consist of making space for stories in the world that have formerly been untold and/or underrepresented.

Through her degree in K-12 Urban Literacy, work with the National Writing Project, her teaching at the 6-12 level as well as the undergraduate and graduate level, Urbanski has witnessed the power shift into the hands of the writer when they are encouraged and trusted to tell their stories with their words.

INVITE CYNTHIA URBANSKI TO SPEAK TO YOUR CLASS OR GROUP!

Connect with her online at cindyurbanski.com or email her at cindy@cindyurbanski.com.

APPENDIXES

APPENDIX A: GEE'S CRITICAL DISCOURSE ANALYSIS

Critical Discourse Analysis (CDA) is concerned with the way language-in-use distributes social goods through the use of the "grammar of our language to take a particular perspective" on the world (Gee, 1999, p. 5). In doing so, language in use marks what is normal or right or valued in the worldview of the speaker. Gee (2010) explains that what is constructed as normal or right has everything to do with the figured world in which the speaker is acting, as well as the intersecting figured worlds or activity systems in dialogue within that world (Kindle location 2039). He also explains these figured worlds as an important point of analysis because "they mediate between the local interactional work" of people and "Discourse [language and everything else] as they operate to create the complex patterns of institutions . . ." (Kindle location 2050).

Fairclough (2003) explains that language has constructive powers and the way people talk about the world forms their common sense notions of it. CDA offers a toolset for mapping the way people are talking about their worlds, analyzing that talk for what is assumed, what is said, what is left out, and what is seen as truth in order to understand what language is attempting to do socially and politically (meaning the distribution of social goods.) Fairclough solidifies the importance of looking at language in critical social research by pointing to it as "a crucial aspect of the social transformations which are going on" within the larger figured world, or activity system. He adds "one cannot make sense of them without thinking about language" (p. 203).

Gee (2010) explains the importance of figured worlds as a tool of inquiry because they serve as a mediating tool between the local (micro) level of human interaction and the institutional (macro) level. He states, "they mediate between the local interactional work we humans do," meaning what language builds, and "Discourses as they operate to create the complex patterns of institutions and cultures across society and history" (p. 76). Gee's focus on language at the micro level enables the analyst to look closely at the way in which language is building the figured world or activity system.

Gee's *seven building tasks* are tools for analyzing the discourses of a particular figured world, and looking at the conversations of that figured world will enable me to situate the language moments in the larger social context and think about how those moments are building the larger social context. For Gee (1999), people use language to build seven things or "seven areas of 'reality'" (p. 17) that come together in the performance of identities and power negotiations within a figured world. These building tasks are significance, practices or activities, identities, relationships, politics or the distribution of social goods, connections, sign systems and knowledge (pp. 17–20). The way language builds these seven areas of reality in terms of what is right and normal in a figured world determines the power structures of the figured world. Gee's CDA asks questions around these seven building tasks in order to analyze the identities that are being constructed and the power negotiations that are happening in a piece of language and thereby how that language is building the figured world or activity system it is operating in.

APPENDIX B: LESLIE'S INTERVIEW IN STANZAS

STANZA I: BECOMING THE TEACHER
1a. Writing, uh,
1b. helps, uh,
2. organize your thoughts and
3. how you felt towards
4a. a certain subject
4b. or topic uh,

STANZA II: BECOMING THE READING SPECIALIST
5a. it, um
5b. it helps you understand
6. the text or what you are reading
7. um, better, but

STANZA III: BECOMING THE GOOD STUDENT
8. writing,
9. writing's good.

APPENDIX C: ERIN'S HOLOCAUST DIARY INTERVIEW IN STANZAS

STANZA I: GOOD STUDENTS CRY, THEY DON'T GET ANGRY
1. I like reading and
2. sometimes I like to cry to

3. get out of

4. to stop being angry.

APPENDIX D: ERIN'S SECOND INTERVIEW IN STANZAS

STANZA I: BEING A GOOD STUDENT
Tell me a little bit about how you guys use this notebook [her daybook] in class.
1. E. Umm sometimes,
2. uh if it's Monday,
3. he says to write about our weekend.
4. Or if we had a spring break or something we have to write about what happened.
5. We had a good time or not.

STANZA II: BEING A WRITER
6. C. Okay.
7. What else do you write in there?
8. E. Ummmm
9. We do a lot of writing in here,
10. I don't really know where it is,
11. but we had to umm either write a story or um
12. just tell what it means.
13. And this is what I wrote [she looks through the notebook and closes it]
13. C. Alright. Is there anything else you want to tell me about your writing in class?
14. Anything in particular I should look at when I start digging through your notebook?
15. E. No

APPENDIX E: ABIGAIL'S FIRST INTERVIEW IN STANZAS

STANZA I: I'M A GOOD STUDENT IN SOCIAL STUDIES.
1. Well,
2. we were writing the diary entries
3. acting like we were African
4. and it makes us feel like we were actually there
5. and we get the experience of how they felt
6. when they were on the ship.

APPENDIX F: ABIGAIL'S SECOND INTERVIEW IN STANZAS

STANZA I: I'M DIFFERENT IN SOCIAL STUDIES AND ENGLISH

1. A. Well, writing in English class,
2. we're doing like essays
3. and then we come in here and we do diary entries,
4. so it's like we do poetry writing, essay writing in [Mr. T's] class,
5. and then we come to [Ronald's] class and we do diary entries and stuff,
6. so it's real different.

APPENDIX G: JADA'S FIRST INTERVIEW IN STANZAS

STANZA I: IT'S JUST SCHOOL

1. J. Okay,
2. I felt like writing this because
3. it was just history and school work
4. and um,

STANZA II: BEING A GOOD SAD STUDENT

5. and I felt sad because,
6. it was people were dying and stuff and
7. they had to wait
8. for the United States and the rest of the countries
9. to get there and get help.

STANZA III: I'M COOL, I CAN DO SCHOOL

10. And
11. I felt like sharing this in school because
12. it was, oh,
13. like me,
14. I'm just like
15. cool and stuff, so I just wanted to share it,
16. just so that they would know I could write it
17. write the diary entries and stuff

STANZA IV: TELL ME ABOUT SCHOOL WORK

18. T. So that your classmates would know?
19. Yeah.
20. So, tell me a little bit more
21. about what you said at the start
22. about it being schoolwork

STANZA V: OH! BOOTSTRAPS AND THE AMERICAN DREAM

23. J. Oh Yeah.
24. It's like,
25. it's like that you should always do your schoolwork
26. and uh always uh, uh, . . .
27. just to do your schoolwork,
28. so that you can get a grade and,
29. and a higher grade
30. so that you will be able to do good in school
31. so that you can go to college.

APPENDIX H: JADA'S SECOND INTERVIEW IN STANZAS

STANZA I: I DIDN'T WANT TO CRY

1. J. Oh I chose this one because
2. I didn't want to cry in front of all them girls
3. so I just wrote about the end
4. and like the part where they came and saved everybody.

STANZA II: "CORRECT ANSWER" YOU WANTED TO BE SAFE

5. C. That makes sense.
6. It makes a lot of sense.
7. So you liked this happier part,
8. it seemed a little safer to write about,
9. I understand that!
10. You did a really great job with it.
11. How do you feel
12. about that piece of writing?

STANZA III: ANSWERING THE QUIZ QUESTION

13. J. I feel good because
14. it was sad.
15. Everybody was crying and stuff
16. and uh, and
17. I felt like writing this uh, uh,
18. hmmmm . . .
19. I don't know why I felt like writing this.
20. I just felt like writing something.
21. I didn't want to do my homework.

STANZA IV: WRONG AGAIN

22. C. Was this homework?
23. J. [nods]

APPENDIX I: QUESTIONS FOR DISCUSSION BETWEEN ADMINISTRATORS, TEACHERS, AND CONSULTANTS

- What are the narratives of learning and schooling present in the figured world of our school and the larger figured world in which our school functions? In what ways are these narratives in conflict with each other and with those of the students? How might we make these conflicting narratives visible and find ways to purposefully and critically negotiate these narratives alongside students, accessing the agency we all have within the figured world of schooling?

- What narrative of literacy do we want to bring forward in our school? Is it a set of skills to be learned? Is it a vehicle by which people can construct and critique the world around them? How do each of these narratives construct students as citizens of the world? How do we ultimately want literacy to function for our students?

- What are the individual needs of the students? What engages them most? Why is that? What narratives are they enacting and how can we honor that in the figured world of our school and classrooms?

- What connections can be made between the funds of knowledge our students possess outside of school and the curriculum we want to teach? How can we leverage those funds of knowledge to make connections to the curriculum in ways that honor what the students already know?

- What of resistant students? How might what is happening in school, and quite possibly the power narrative, be constructing these students in a way with which they are uncomfortable? What critique on the system of schooling might they be offering? How can we use literacy to help the students voice that critique in productive and empowering ways?

REFERENCES

Adichie, C. N. (2009). *The danger of a single story.* TED Talks. Retrieved from https://www.ted.com/talks/chimamanda_adichie_the_danger_of_a_single_story?language=en

Anyon, J. (1997). Ghetto schooling: A political economy of urban educational reform. New York, NY: Teachers College Press.

Ayers, R., & Ayers, W. (2011). *Teaching the taboo.* New York, NY: Teachers College Press.

Bakhtin, M. M. (1981). Discourse in the novel. In M. Holquist (Ed.), *The dialogic imagination: Four essays by M. M. Bakhtin* (pp. 258–422). (C. Emerson and M. Holquist, Trans.). Austin, TX: University of Texas Press.

Bettie, J. (2003). *Women without class: Girls, race and identity.* Berkeley, CA: University of California Press.

Bourdieu, P., & Passeron, J. (1990). *Reproduction in education, society and culture* (2nd ed). Thousand Oaks, CA: Sage Publications.

Brannon, L., Courtney, J. & Urbanski, C. (2008) The five-paragraph essay and the deficit model of education. *English Journal 98*(2), 16–21.

Brannon, L., Griffin, S., Haag, K., Iannone, T., Urbanski, C., & Woodward, S. (2008). *Thinking out loud on paper: The student daybook as a tool to foster learning.* Portsmouth, NH: Heinemann.

Brannon, L., & Scott, T. (2013). Democracy, struggle, and the praxis of assessment. *College Composition and Communication, 62*(2), 273-298.

Bulcock, J. W., Whitt, M. E., & Beebe, M. J. (1991). Gender differences, student well-being and high school achievement. *Alberta Journal of Educational Research, 37,* 209–224.

DeMitchell, T. A. (2006). School uniforms: There is no free lunch [Electronic version]. *Teachers College Record.* Retrieved Nov. 2015 from http://www.tcrecord.org/Content.asp?ContentID=12891

Engestrom, Y., & Miettinen, R. (1999). .*Perspectives on activity theory.* Y. Engestrom, R. Miettinen, & R. Punamaki (Eds.),. Cambridge, MA: Cambridge University Press.

Epstein, D., Elwood, J., Jey, V., & Maw, J. (1998). *Failing boys? Issues in gender and achievement.* Buckingham, PA: Open University Press.

Fairclough, N. (2003). *Analyzing discourse: Textual analysis for social research.* New York, NY: Routledge.

Foucault, M. (1977). *Discipline & punish: The birth of the prison.* New York, NY: Vintage Books.

Foucault, M. (1980). *Power/knowledge: Selected interviews & other writings 1972–1977.* C. Gordon (Ed.). (C. Gordon, L. Marshall, J. Mepham, K. Soper, Trans.). New York, NY: Pantheon Books.

Freire, P. (1997). *Pedagogy of the oppressed.* New York, NY: Continuum.

Freudenthaler, H. H., Spinath, B., & Neubauer, A. C. (2008). Predicting school achievement in boys and girls. *European Journal of Personality, 22*(3), 231–245.

Gallagher, C. (2011). Being there: (Re)making the assessment scene. *College Composition and Communication, 62*(3), 450–476.

Gee, J. P. (1989). Literacy, discourse, and linguistics: Introduction and what is literacy? In E. Cushman, E. Kintgen, B. M. Kroll, & M. Rose (Eds.), *Literacy: A critical sourcebook* (pp. 525–544). New York, NY: Bedford/St. Martins.

Gee, J. P. (1999). *An introduction to discourse analysis: Theory and method* (2nd ed.). New York, NY: Routledge.

Gee, J. P. (2010). *An introduction to discourse analysis: Theory and method* (3rd ed.). New York, NY: Routledge.

Gee, J. P. (2011). Identity as an analytic lens for research in education. *Review of Research in Education 25,* 99–125.

Giroux, H. (1983). *Theory & resistance in education: A pedagogy for the opposition.* New York, NY: Bergin & Garvey.

Hess, F. M. & Petrilli, M. J. (2007). *No Child Left Behind primer.* New York: Peter Lang.

Holland, D., Lachicotte, W., Skinner, D., & Cain, C. (1998). *Identity and agency in cultural worlds.* Cambridge, MA: Harvard University Press.

Joseph, N. (1986). *Uniforms and nonuniforms: Communication through clothing.* Westport, CT: Greenwood.

Kaiser, S. B. (1985). *The social psychology of clothing and personal adornment.* New York, NY: Macmillan.

Kamberelis, G., & Dimitriadis, G. (2005). *Qualitative inquiry: Approaches to language and literacy research.* New York, NY: Teachers College Press.

Kohn, A. (1998). *What to look for in a classroom . . . and other essays.* San Francisco, CA: Josey-Bass.

Luke, A. (1992). The body literate: Discourse and inscription in early literacy training. *Linguistics and Education 4,* 107–129.

Lyotard, J. F. (1979). *The postmodern condition: A report on knowledge.* Minneapolis, MN: University of Minnesota Press.

No Child Left Behind Act of 2001, August 6, 2002. http://www.k12.wa.us/esea/NCLB.aspx

North Carolina Department of Public Instruction. (2008). *Accountability Services Division.* Retrieved from http://www.dpi.state.nc.us/accountability/testing/writing/writingpilot.

Public Schools of North Carolina, Accountability Division. Retrieved Nov. 2015 from http://www.dpi.state.nc.us/accountability/testing/shared/testdevprocess

Russakoff, D. (2015). *The prize: Who's in charge of America's schools?* New York, NY: Houghton Mifflin Harcourt.

Russell, D. (1995). Activity Theory and its implications for writing instruction. In J. Petraglia (Ed.), *Reconceiving writing, rethinking writing instruction* (pp. 51–77). New York, NY: Routledge.

Ryan, J. (1991). Observing and normalizing: Foucault, discipline, and inequality in schooling: Big brother is watching you. *The Journal of Educational Thought (JET) / Revue De La Pensée Éducative, 25*(2), 104–119.

Stanley, M. S. (1996). School uniforms and safety. *Education and Urban Society, 28*(4), 424–435.

Urbanski, C. D. (2006). *Using the workshop approach in the high school English classroom: Modeling effective writing, reading, and thinking strategies for student success.* Thousand Oaks, CA: Corwin Press.

Van Houtte, M. (2004). Why boys achieve less at school than girls: The differences between boys' and girls' academic culture. *Educational Studies, 30*, 159–173.

Vygotsky, L. S. (1978). *Mind in society: The Development of higher psychological processes.* Cambridge, MA: Harvard University Press.

Wong, K.-C., Lam, Y. R., & Ho, L.-M. (2002). The effects of schooling on gender differences. *British Educational Research Journal, 28*, 827–843.

Yeung, R. (2009). Are school uniforms a good fit? Results from the ECLS-K and the NELS. *Educational Policy, 23*(6), 847–874.

INDEX

Abigail (student), 93–98, 114, 115–116, 125–126
Accessorizing policy, 41–42, 45, 49–50
Accountability. *See* Testing and accountability narrative
Achieve3000 writing program
    adoption of, 11
    competing narratives about, 67–69
    repeating back what you are given, 36, 84
    teacher identity and, 66
    testing and accountability narrative and, 116
    Writing Program narrative and, 28, 32
Activity systems, 44
Activity theory, 43–50, 123
Adichie, Chimamanda Ngozi, 14
After-school time, 82, 86–87
Agency, 111, 116–118
American Dream narrative, 107
Anger versus crying, 89
Anyon, Jean, 119
Argument-only writing policy, 11, 28, 64
Assessments, 118–119. *See also* Testing and accountability narrative
Ayers, R., 64
Ayers, W., 64

"Bad" students (Jada), 101–111, 114, 116, 117, 120, 126–128
Bakhtin, M. M., 83
Banking concept of learning, 23. *See also* Rote learning
Beacon on the hill metaphor, 9, 19
Bell, T. H., 12
Bettie, J., 65, 66, 116
Boehner, Joe, 13
Booker, Cory, 8
Bourdieu, P., 22
Branded marketing, 48–49
Building tasks, 124
Bush administration (Bush II), 13

Cain, C., 20–21, 45, 65, 66, 67, 111

Carceral society, 22, 65
Carter, Dr., 10, 15, 33–35
CDA. *See* Critical discourse analysis (CDA)
Charter schools, 118
Christie, Chris, 8
Clinton, Bill, 12
Code switching, 66
College and Career Readiness Standards, 13
Commodification
    uniformity of instruction and, 52, 54–55
    of writing, 72–73, 84–86, 96–97
Common Core State Standards (CCSS), 11, 13–14
Compliance narrative, 55, 64–65
Control. *See* Order and control narrative
Convergent narratives, 71
Covey, Stephen M. R., 1–2
Creativity
    accessorizing and, 48
    not allowed by students, 38, 81, 102–104
    of teachers, 52, 65, 74, 76
Critical discourse analysis (CDA), 81–82, 123–124. *See also* Abigail; Erin; Jada; Leslie
Critical thinking
    "good" at-risk students and, 86
    rote learning versus, 3, 74
    by teachers, 66
    testing and accountability not valuing, 37–38
Crying, 89, 108

"The Danger of a Single Story" (Adichie), 14
Daybook writing
    Abigail, 94
    activities using, 26–27
    defined, 26
    Erin, 91–92
    gender and, 80
    Leslie, 83
    Ronald using, 72–75, 80
Deadbeat teachers, 66
Deficit views
    beacon on the hill metaphor and, 9

uniforms and, 48
    urban school reform and, 14
    writing types and, 27–28
Delinquency, carceral society and, 22
Democratization, professional development and, 15
Dialectic Journals, 27
Dialogic teaching, 23
Diary writing
    Abigail, 94–95
    Erin, 87–89
    Holocaust diary writing, 69–72, 80, 102–111
    impacts of, 61–62
    Jada, 102–111
Differentiation, 54
Dimitriadis, G., 44
Discourse identity (D-identity). *See also* "Bad"
    students (Jada); "Good" at-risk students
    defined, 67
    Leslie, 83
    performance and, 116
    success and, 118, 128–129
    use of, 81
Discourses, 44
Double Entry Journals, 27
Duncan, Arne, 13

Educational policy, trust and, 1. *See also Specific*
    policies and reforms
Education reform, 12. *See also* Urban school reform
Eidman-Aadah, Elyse, 1–2
Elementary and Secondary Education Act, 12
Erin (student), 69, 86–93, 97–98, 114, 115, 125
Every Student Succeeds Act, 2

Fairclough, N., 123
Falsely passing, 111
Figured worlds. *See also* Order and control narrative;
    Resistance narrative; Socialization narrative;
    Testing and accountability narrative
    activity theory and, 45–46, 123
    commodification of writing and, 72–73, 84–86,
        96–97
    outsiders and, 24, 75–76
    overview, 20–21, 45
    urban school reform and, 82, 84, 90, 96, 113
Formulaic writing, 27–28, 36, 62–63, 115. *See also*
    Achieve3000 writing program
Foucault, M., 21, 22, 37, 44, 64, 65
Free time, 82, 86–87

Gallagher, C., 119, 121
Gee, James Paul, 65, 67, 81–82, 123–124
Gender issues, 80
Genre writing, 61–63. *See also* Daybook writing;
    Diary writing
Giroux, Henry, 22, 64
"Good" at-risk students
    Abigail, 93–98, 114, 115–116, 125–126
    creativity not recognized as, 104
    deficit views, 81
    Erin, 69, 86–93, 97–98, 114, 115, 125
    gender and, 80
    interview questions for, 79
    Leslie, 82–86, 97–98, 114, 115, 124
"Good teachers," 73–76

Hero/martyr teachers, 66, 70–71, 75
Hess, F. M., 12, 13
Hidden curriculum, 22
Holland, D., 20–21, 45, 65, 66, 67, 111
Holocaust diary writing, 69–72, 80, 102–111

Identity construction, 65–67, 83, 86, 116
Improvisation, 66–67, 102, 107, 111
Institutional identity (I-identity), 66, 81, 83. *See also*
    "Good" at-risk students
Intervention plans, 25

Jada (student), 101–111, 114, 116, 117, 120, 126–
    128

Kamberelis, G., 44
Kennedy, Ted, 13

Labels, 65
Lachicotte, W., 20–21, 45, 65, 66, 67, 111
Learning Focused School (LFS) curriculum, 10–11,
    30–32
Leontiev, A., 43, 45
Leslie (student), 82–86, 97–98, 114, 115, 124
Lexile levels, 11
Luke, A., 120
Lyotard, J.-F., 117

Mediating tools, 45, 52
Meir, Deborah, 119
Membershipping, 66, 71
Monitoring, of students and teachers, 34, 50, 53, 68

Morgan, Mrs., 9, 10–11, 15, 35, 50

Narratives, single stories and, 14
National Commission on Excellence in Education, 12
National Writing Project (NWP), 9–10, 23–24, 114–116
A Nation at Risk report, 12
No Child Left Behind (NCLB), 1, 2, 13
Normalizing institutions, 37
Normalizing narrative, 37

Obama administration, 13
Order and control narrative
    free time and, 82
    as illusion, 55–56
    over student movement and noise, 24, 33–34, 42
    planning matrix and, 42–43, 50–55
    student resistance to, 41–42, 45, 49–50
    teacher resistance to, 54–55, 64–65, 117
    uniforms and, 33, 37, 41–42, 47–50
Orderliness as valued, 33–34, 35, 71
Outsider status, 24, 75–76

Pacing guides, 15, 74–75
Passeron, J., 22
Passing, 65, 66–67, 87, 111
Performativity, 116–117
Petrilli, M. J., 12, 13
Planning matrix, 42–43, 45, 50–55
Play writing, 64
Poverty, 42, 119
Power narrative
    discourses and, 44–45
    dominant ideology and, 22, 117–118
    research needed on, 120
    social positioning and, 24
    testing industry and, 53–54
    uniforms and, 49–50
    view of teachers and, 114
    winners and losers in, 121
    Writing Program narrative and, 114–116
The Prize (Russakoff), 8
Professional development (PD), 10, 15, 23, 52–53

Quick Writes, 27

Race to the Top initiative, 13
Reagan administration, 12
Regimes of truth, 21

Remembering the Holocaust, 69–70
Resistance narrative
    "bad" students and, 101–111
    as critique of system, 113
    daybook writing and, 75
    need for, 121
    socialization and, 117
    teachers and, 54–55, 64–65, 117
    testing and accountability and, 119
    uniform policy and, 41–42, 45, 49–50
Rigorous writing workshops, 28–30
Ronald (teacher)
    daybook writing, 72–75, 80
    identity and, 66, 67
    leaving school, 114, 118
    resistance by, 64, 76
Rosa Parks Middle School. *See also* "Good" at-risk students; Order and control narrative; Power narrative; Resistance narrative; Testing and accountability narrative; Urban school reform
    administrators' perspective on, 33–36
    atmosphere of, 24–25
    "bad" students, 101–111, 114, 116, 117, 120, 126–128
    competing narratives about, 15, 20–22, 36–38, 114–116
    National Writing Project at, 9–12
    overview, 9
    physical structure of, 19–20
    testing and accountability at, 14
    uniform policy at, 33, 37, 41–42, 44–50
    urban school reform story at, 8
    Writing Program perspective on, 22–33
Rote learning
    critical thinking versus, 3, 74
    giving back what you are told, 81, 82–83, 102
Russakoff, D., 8
Russell, D., 44
Ryan, J., 64

Safe and Orderly School designation, 33
Samuel (teacher), 66, 69–72, 76, 113–114
School uniforms, 33, 37, 41–42, 44–50, 82
Scripted lessons, 15
Seven building tasks, 124
Single stories, 14
Skinner, D., 20–21, 45, 65, 66, 67, 111
Socialization narrative
    Foucault and, 64

"good" at-risk students and, 22, 97
  mediating tools and, 45
  order and control narrative and, 55
  resistance and, 117
Social reproduction
  carceral society and, 22
  defined, 8
  planning matrix and, 42–43, 45
  school uniforms and, 45–50
  testing and accountability and, 8, 14, 22,
    113–116
Speed of trust, 1–2
Standards, 12. *See also Specific standards*
Student interviews. *See* "Good" at-risk students; Jada
  (student)
Subjects, 44
Success, questions to discuss about discourse identity
  of, 128–129
Summary, Response, Connection, 27
Summer institutes, 10

Teacher consultants (TCs), 10
Teachers, informal interactions between, 54
Teach for America teachers, 114
Testing and accountability narrative
  charter schools and, 118
  focus on, 35–36
  formulaic writing and, 27–28, 36, 62–63, 115
  parental role and, 119, 120
  planning and the testing industry, 53–54
  resistance to, 119
  at Rosa Parks Middle School, 14
  social reproduction and, 8, 14, 22, 113–116
  as standard, 21
  teacher identity and, 66
  uniformity as good, 43
  urban school reform and, 8, 9, 12–14, 37–38,
    113
Theory-in-use, 80
Tonita, J., 1
Trust, 1–2, 10, 23–24
Truth claims, 21

Uniformity as good, 50–52
Uniforms, 33, 37, 41–42, 44–50, 82
Unstructured after-school time, 82, 86–87
Urban school reform
  activity theory and, 45–46
  complexity of, 22

deficit views and, 14
  "good teachers" and, 76
  narrative of, 8
  normalizing narrative and, 37
  teacher role in, 55
  testing and accountability and, 8, 9, 12–14,
    37–38, 113
  Truth claims and, 21
  uniforms and, 48, 82
Urban schools, stereotypes of, 7–8

Ventriloquating, 83
Vygotsky, L., 43–44

Women Without Class (Bettie), 116
Writer's notebooks. *See* Daybook writing
Writing, as mediating tool versus outcome, 68
Writing into the Day, 27

Youth Roots, 119–120

Zones of proximal development, 43–44
Zuckerberg, Mark, 8